International Motor Racing
Book 4

'HAPPINESS IS A SQUARE-SHAPED FLAG'

Man with the chequered flag has a wide grin for Brian Redman who lets go the steering wheel of hi Porsche in delight as he wins the BOAC 500 6-Hour Sports Car Race at Brands Hatch. Redman' co-driver was Jo Siffert.

INTERNATIONAL MOTOR RACING BOOK 4

Edited by Phil Drackett

with contributions by

JACKIE STEWART

BRUCE McLAREN   JACK BRABHAM   DENNY HULME

CHRIS AMON   EOIN YOUNG

EDDIE GUBA   AL BOCHROCH   ALAN BRINTON

MARK KAHN   GRAHAM MACBETH

JOAN DRACKETT   BUZZ BARRE   RON NAYLOR

SOUVENIR PRESS LTD · LONDON

First published by Souvenir Press Ltd., London, W.1. and
simultaneously in Canada by The Ryerson Press, Toronto, 2.

ISBN 0 285 50258 1

Printed in Great Britain by
Bookprint Limited, Crawley, Sussex

CONTENTS

CONTENTS—*continued*

LIST OF ILLUSTRATIONS

Photographs by Gerry Stream, Ron Ockenden, Nigel Snowdon, Ford, Fred Taylor, Diana Burnett, William Cook, Trojan, Eoin Young, Roger Hall, Al Bochroch, Barry M. Tenin, Geoffrey Goddard, Rank, Shell, Autocar, John Whitmore, Daily Graphic, Motor, A. V. Swaebe, Autosport, Penelope Griffiths, Peter Roderick, The Royal Automobile Club.

'THE VILLAIN WAS A HARD CASE'

Jackie Stewart had earned pole position for the RAC British Grand Prix when he crashed and was lucky to escape injury. The culprit was—this piece of concrete which broke loose from the track and caused Jackie's car to go off. But Jackie won the race—despite having to drive a strange car.

9

What happens to a man when he achieves a life's ambition? What does he think, what does he feel when that moment comes along when the universe is at his feet, when hundreds of thousands acclaim him? Some folk win the football pools, some gain Nobel Prizes, some become big business tycoons. Jackie Stewart, from that Anglo-Scottish Border Country where they seem to spawn drivers as readily as salmon, won the World Driver's Championship in 1969. In an exclusive interview, he tells Phil Drackett just how it feels to be champion.

I WAS VERY HAPPY WHEN I WON AT MONZA

DRACKETT: What was the most exciting moment of the 1969 racing season for you?

STEWART: Well, I suppose obviously the most exciting moment was the reality of winning Monza and the World Championship. The trouble with motor racing from my point of view is that usually I'm completely drained of emotion after I've won a race—or even lost a race. I seem to have been mentally and physically at my peak for, let's say, two hours and the reality of success or failure doesn't seem to touch me for quite a long time. I was very happy when I won Monza. I can remember driving into, well not into but alongside the pits and my wife, Helen, and Ken Tyrrell and everyone else coming out to me. I can remember thinking—well, I've won the World Championship and I've won Monza and

it's happened the way I wanted it. It couldn't have been better than to win the title by taking the decisive race rather than being placed. But it wasn't until the next morning, in fact, that I fully realised I was World Champion and perhaps all the things it was going to mean to me by personal pleasure, satisfaction, etcetera.

DRACKETT: What was the closest and the toughest race of the year as far as you were concerned?

STEWART: One of the most difficult races was Silverstone (the British Grand Prix) because it was a real good dice from start to finish with Jochen Rindt. I had a minor problem in the car, very minor. I had done reasonably well in practice and had held pole position for most of the time. Then close to the end of practice that piece of concrete came out of the road to write my own car off from the race and I had to take over Jean-Pierre Beltoise's car. In reality I still held the pole position with my own car but, of course, since there was no alternative to withdrawing it as it was so badly damaged, I had to establish a new time with Jean-Pierre's car very quickly. His car, of course, wasn't set up for me at all, driving-position wise, or suspension wise. To then put up what was second fastest time in practice made me very happy with myself. I was even more happy to win the race in this different motor car. During the race, it was a close dice all the way with Jochen and a race I enjoyed very much because it was tooth-and-nail. I am just sorry that he finally dropped out because things would have got pretty interesting. I had started to put on some pressure just at that time and had put in three or four very quick laps, the quickest laps of my race, and this was at the point where I think we would have both had to pull out our maximum effort.

DRACKETT: Rindt really had to drop out at the point of maximum interest?

STEWART: Yes, my car was just about at the right fuel load to have a real go at his car and I'd just started in fact to put up my fastest lap in the race.

DRACKETT: Which cars and drivers did you think were the strongest opposition of 1969?

STEWART: The man who was consistently a concern to me was Jochen. Yes, Jochen Rindt and the Lotus were the most formidable opposition of 1969. Jacky Ickx on occasions but never to the same extent as Jochen. Jochen was consistently there where Jacky would come in at places like the Nürburgring and put up a very good performance.

DRACKETT: Do you think Jochen will be a threat again?

STEWART: Oh yes, I think he would be the man I'd have to beat again. If there was only one man to choose then I think he would be the man who would be most difficult, but, of course, there's Jack Brabham and Jacky Ickx and Chris Amon and people of that calibre as well as Graham Hill I hope, and

Denny Hulme, you know there's too many of them —that's the trouble. If there was just one I wouldn't mind but the spearhead of that group, let's say, would have to be Jochen.

DRACKETT: What do you think were the most important factors in your Championship year, both as far as you personally were concerned, and from the point of car and team?

STEWART: I think we were so well prepared for the season. Ken Tyrrell had put together an extremely reliable group of people right from the mechanics who, I think, gave me a better prepared car than any other Grand Prix driver had. In a way we had done our homework. We'd gone to all the tracks ahead of time with Dunlop and had put in a tremendous amount of tyre testing and development work in that field. And I think the Matra. The chassis was strong and reliable and this was of major importance. I think the car could have been better but, you know, they always can be better and I was very happy.

DRACKETT: Every part of the car is obviously of importance but what degree of priority would you give to engine, driver and so on?

STEWART: First of all, we've got to regard the Ford engine as being absolutely essential. This has supplied the success I've been looking for because, in my case, it's been very reliable, indeed for the whole team, it's been very reliable. I think then if I were to put things in priority I would say the engine, the tyres, the driver and the chassis. I put the chassis last not because I don't think it's important but because it's fairly obvious to anyone who studies the results, the starting-grids and the performances that on many, many occasions there has been perhaps a variety of four different makes on the front line of any starting-grid and this would mean that the difference between these cars is only a fraction of a second because the drivers themselves are all capable. We're all using exactly the same engine but the tyres can save a second, half a second, more than a second in some cases if someone comes out with a new development and a driver must be able to take advantage of his good tyres or his good chassis. His

Jackie Stewart chased by Graham Hill in the Italian Grand Prix at Monza. Stewart's win over Rindt and Beltoise in this race clinched the World Championship.

engine he must accept to be the same. So I would put the driver in fact only third in the list.

DRACKETT: I noticed the other day that you had been in South Africa testing tyres and Jack Brabham was quoted as saying that he didn't like South Africa for testing tyres. He's on a different tyre, of course, isn't he?

STEWART: Yes, he's running on Goodyear. I find South Africa fine for various reasons. First of all, one cannot regard any circuit as being perfect for one's tyre testing for the season. You've got to accept that you've got to go to all of the circuits to get a tyre to suit that particular character of track. South Africa, from our point of view, has continuity of weather which, of course, California and other places have too but the track itself offers a variety of different kinds of corners, slow corners, fast corners, braking corners, change-of-direction corners, almost every type of corner that you're likely to come up against

and perhaps show some weakness in a tyre construction, compound or design. I find it extremely good to analyse my tyre or my car on that track because there is also a straight—a thinking space—between each corner. One must be able to go round a corner and analyse the behaviour of the car or tyre on that corner after you have completed it. If you are going to test tyres or car I personally feel that you have to test them at ten-tenths or nine-tenths. I don't think you can ever take a car to, let's say, six-tenths and then say that you think the car or the tyre is good. You must be at absolute maximum to be able to reproduce race conditions and therefore you must be able—after you've gone round a corner—to condense and collect your thoughts, analyse them and pick out the things which cropped up. You must recall the good or the bad during the brief fraction of a second before you get ready for braking and the next corner and this is where I find South Africa very good.

13

Stewart practising for the Dutch Grand Prix in the four-wheel drive Matra. He drove a conventional two-wheel drive car to victory in the race itself.

DRACKETT: Which Grand Prix race or circuit is your preference?

STEWART: Monte Carlo's got lovely hotels and restaurants. Monza's got the Villa de Esté on Como and you can't beat that. I don't know. I've tried to stop myself having real favourites among the racing tracks, if you know what I mean.

DRACKETT: You think you can develop a complex about some tracks?

STEWART: I suppose you can. I can't say—I wouldn't be able to say, truthfully, that I'm a man in love with Spa. But not because of my accident there. I've led the race twice, I've finished second—and I'd love to win it—but because of its unforgiveness, because of its character, because of its venue, I suppose, I certainly wouldn't class it as my favourite. However, it is still a very demanding course. The Nürburgring when I am sitting at home

—I think I've said this before—is very good. It's something else, it's an enormous challenge. I don't know, I think I like Clermont. It offers a variety of corners in about the right length of track, you know it's not a little Nürburgring, it's 5.1 miles and it's got 51 corners of varying types. Perhaps it's a little narrow but it's still a big challenge.

DRACKETT: You must be the first World Champion in the history of the sport to follow up his Championship year by driving a car yet to make its début on the race circuit. Why do you think this gamble is justified because it surely must be a gamble?

STEWART: Well, again it is perhaps because of my analysis of the four things I already spoke of, of the engine, of the tyres, of the drivers and of the chassis. The chassis is important to the point where it must be reliable, must not be so unconventional or futuristic that it becomes fragile or very troublesome but

at the same time it's got to be modern. Robin Herd is one of the best racing designers at this time and a very practical man but Ken Tyrrell is even more practical and with Ken's watching eye, the March can be a very successful chassis. And with the Ford engine and Dunlop tyres I feel that I'm justified in being, if not optimistic, which a Scotsman can't be, at least with some confidence going into the new season.

DRACKETT: In other words your first three factors are exactly the same. It is the fourth factor which is the unknown quantity?

STEWART: Of course—and it's a very important factor because it must be a strong car and a reliable one. It must be able to hold the road and run well and in this I am relying on Robin Herd and his group of designers.

DRACKETT: What's your immediate ambition?

STEWART: To be World Champion again.

DRACKETT: What are your long-term ambitions?

STEWART: In motor sport to remain in it for many more years and to be able to choose my time for retiring. To have a happy family which I think is more important than most things and perhaps anything else. For my own personal future beyond motor racing, of this I'm not sure because almost every six months I see something new, some other opportunity that I didn't see six months ago, because today I travel so much and get so many wonderful chances of seeing new things and getting new opportunities so that what I thought was really right six months ago might not be true today and of course might not be true six months hence.

DRACKETT: Do you think basically that you would like to stay with something connected with motoring?

STEWART: Right now I think not. I don't know. When I finish motor racing I like to think that I'll wake up one morning and say, 'I just don't understand why I've been enthusiastic about this.' You know I'm going to get out of it and I'll no longer have the urge; I won't be a lost racing driver feeling that he wants to go back—I hope. I hope I'll be tired of it. And I hope that I won't tire of it over a period. I hope that one morning I'll just feel sick of it and stop. Now this happened with my shooting when I was doing that and it was a very happy ending to an affair.

DRACKETT: Talking of the family, would you like to see your sons become racing drivers?

STEWART: I'm very selfish. I'm a very selfish loving father and to see my sons motor racing having been involved in it myself and knowing the life that one leads I'm sure they might be happy doing it but I would like to see them doing something else. That's of course being very selfish.

DRACKETT: What advice would you give to an aspiring racing driver?

STEWART: He wants to be sure first of all that he has something in life where he has an anchor—some profession—and his education must be finished. It's not necessary that he starts being a racing driver at 17 or 19 or 20 years of age. I didn't start until I was 22 or 23 and I don't think it's done me a lot of harm. To have his education, to have his profession fully established, that allows him to go out with some freedom of mind. He's not completely wasting his opportunity if motor racing is unkind to him. Motor racing can be the most generous, happy existence in

15

Stewart (Matra) in action during the RAC British Grand Prix which he won after a miraculous escape from injury during practice.

Even Grand Prix drivers sometimes get a moment for relaxation. Jackie Stewart (above), complete with waders and deer-stalker, prepares for the first cast of the morning as he goes in chase of some native salmon. Jackie (below), is serenaded by Chris Barber and his band at Brands Hatch. In the absence of rain or sun, the purpose of the umbrella is unknown!

the world but it also can be a very cruel one and a very difficult one to live with. One must be able to do this with the thought in mind that all is not lost if things do not go well. Opportunities occur in motor racing and when the opportunities happen sometimes you're not there and if you're not there to pick up that piece that's been dropped it might never be dropped again. So it's a very chancy profession in that respect. But also, you know, a wonderful one.

DRACKETT: Which is the car you have most enjoyed driving and who would you consider to be the outstanding driver on the Grand Prix circuit during the time you have been racing?

STEWART: The Matra MS80 is the nicest car I drove last year and that I've ever driven. As for drivers, Jim Clark undoubtedly.

DRACKETT: What would you regard as your finest win?

STEWART: The '68 German Grand Prix. As a second, Clermont Ferrand in '69 because I felt I drove that race as I wanted to.

DRACKETT: Would I be wrong in thinking that you haven't had many disastrous races, near squeaks and so on except for the Spa one?

STEWART: I've had the odd scratch and the odd brush with mistakes and bits and pieces but I must say that I've been very fortunate and a lot of this is due to the preparation that I've had in all of my motor-racing career. The cars that I've driven have all been very well put together cars and this has a lot to do with things.

DRACKETT: You'd really say that homework has got to be number one?

STEWART: Yes, and of course, you've obviously got to be very fortunate.

'You can easily beat yourself'

says BRUCE McLAREN

SO many people have asked me how it is that McLaren Racing can keep winning Can-Am races, that I've given the matter a lot of thought and while I can't come up with any simple answer, it has occurred to me that we're winning Can-Am sports car races in North America for the same reasons that the Cosworth-Ford 3-litre DFV engines are dominating Grand Prix racing. Like us, Cosworth don't do anything out of the ordinary. They use piston engines with four valves per cylinder, and there have been four-valve heads around since the '20s. So there's nothing new in the concept. The fuel cooling device on their engine is new, but it comes from the same logical, sensible, sit-down-and-think-about-it sort of engineering as the fuel system in our Can-Am cars. We could have mounted up a complicated series of pipes and pumps, but we chose the simplest, most basic solution, with one-way valves which let gravity get on with the job.

We reckon that you can easily beat yourself instead of the opposition if you try to get too technical too quickly. Of course you have to keep abreast of all the new developments, but that doesn't mean you have to incorporate every new development in your car just because it's new.

The basic design of our Can-Am sports cars came originally from the tubular-frame Coopers but since then there has been so much development and improvement that when someone else wants to build a Can-Am car they virtually have to copy us, and they lack the tremendous background of research and development that we have slaved through. And if they are just copying blindly, they can make mistakes.

We are working on our new Indianapolis car, as I write, and this is a very specialised event that we have never run in before. The place reeks in tradition and it's a whole new ball game. We looked at Indy cars and it was tempting to copy existing ideas, but in my opinion to copy for the sake of copying would land us in big trouble. If we're going to copy, we should find out why so-and-so did it that way, do an experiment to find out why, and THEN go ahead and borrow the idea. In short, this is just plain good engineering, and this is the basic reason that our cars are good. They're well engineered.

We've also got a team of excellent people who are the right age, who were brought together at the right time, and who all contribute tremendously to the programme. Experience also counts for a lot. I've been through this whole development scene with rear-engined racing cars from the first Cooper days. There are a hundred and one things that you almost forget you ever knew until you see somebody doing something and you think 'Hell, we made that mistake in 1959!' You tend to forget that bank of experience is always there.

So I won the Can-Am Championship for the second time in three years because our car was basically sound and uncomplicated, we had good people, and we have a lot of experience that can't just be bought or traded. I'm also aware that perhaps some of our competitors weren't as successful as we had expected. The Chaparral threat never materialised, and Ford never really made up their mind what they wanted to do in the Can-Am field and only came in at the last minute with an 8-litre aluminium engine for Mario Andretti.

'READY FOR THE OFF'

A study in grim determination. The probing camera of William Cook focuses on Bruce McLaren as the New Zealand ace awaits the starting flag at Watkins Glen, USA. The Glen Can-Am was the third in the series of races which turned out to be a bonanza benefit for the McLaren cars driven by Bruce himself and fellow-Kiwi and former World Champion, Denny Hulme. Between them they won all eleven races in the series.

I think a small company like Lola could become very competitive in Can-Am racing, but I don't think a colossus like Ford will ever make it unless they employ the right sort of people and let them get on with it.

Automobile racing right now is an extremely specialised activity and engineering is an extremely specialised activity. But whereas an engineering graduate will be specialised in some particular field, be it electronics, metallurgy, etc., this will only apply to one small part of the car. The typical college graduate now has very few opportunities to get the broad base of experience that will allow him to design and develop a racing car. He could be part of a team, but it would inevitably wind up being a sort of 'committee car'. The sort of valuable experience that Jack Brabham, Colin Chapman and I were lucky enough to get growing up with the industry is very difficult to get now that industry is so well established.

Where does a young engineer start now? Nobody races Austin 7s like they used to, but Colin Chapman did, and I did. I've always said that a designer who

has a college degree and has raced his own Austin 7, is going to be a beauty, but the guy who has his college degree and is specialised only in thermo dynamics or something, just isn't going to get the job done in the overall area of racing cars, no matter how brilliant he might be in the field of space-age technology.

Look at the American moon project. Great. Tremendous technology involved. But then you go back and you consider the experience of the man behind it all, Von Braun, who was blowing his fingers off with tiny rockets in the late '20s. Ford as a company won't be able to do it in the Can-Am series unless they employ this sort of man, and let that sort of man—someone like Jack Brabham—have enough power so that he could do it his way without someone watching over his shoulder all the time. Then they could do it.

We used 7-litre aluminium 630-horsepower Chevrolet engines again in 1969, but we oh-so-nearly threw our lot in with Ford. By a dead lucky flash of intuition we figured out that the Ford engine was liable to be late and also, if we were to apply

what experience we had with this type of engine to developing the Ford, we would only be creating competitors for ourselves. With the Chevrolet engines only Roger Penske or Jim Hall were using the lightweight engines or were able to afford them, and since we were already competing against them anyway, it seemed logical to stick with the Chevvy. Boy, am I glad we did!

I think probably in 1968 we were able to channel a lot of the lessons we learned from Grand Prix racing into the development of the M8A Can-Am cars, but in 1969 the exchange of information between Grand Prix and Can-Am seemed to even itself out.

We were able to gain an advantage from the Grand Prix development of wings when we fitted the M8B with a big wing, but for instance, when we designed the M15 Indianapolis car we probably applied more knowledge from the Can-Am sports cars than we did from the M7 Grand Prix cars. The M8 sports car was, in fact, a much better car in terms of design than the M7 Grand Prix single-seater, because the M7 was basically a copy of our Formula 2 car and that was never very good. We have also found that the rub-off on information works full circle, and we are able to incorporate ideas and components from the Indy car into our 1970 Can-Am sports cars. . . .

I find there is almost as big a challenge from building a successful racing car as there is in actually sitting behind the wheel and winning the race with it. Well, not quite, but you know what I mean. Racing for some people is a way of releasing all their pent-up energies and emotions, but for me it's more of an engineering exercise.

21

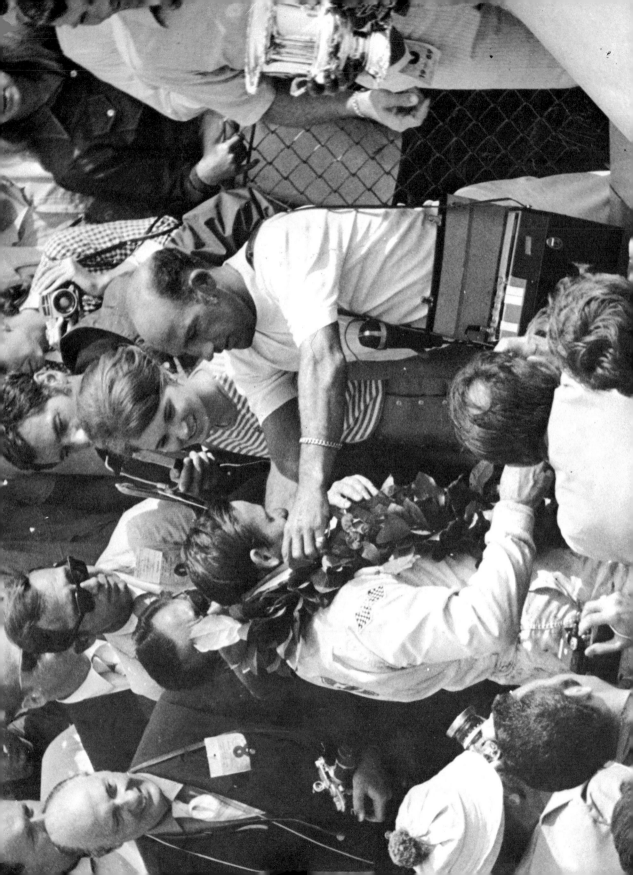

I was half-way through an engineering degree at university in Auckland when I was awarded the 'Driver to Europe' racing scholarship which paid my way over here in 1958, so my racing career has really been a sort of practical extension of my engineering studies.

We signed Denny Hulme and Chris Amon to drive our cars at Indianapolis—nothing like all us Kiwis sticking together—but we tried to get Chris to sign on for Formula 1 as well. This would have meant that I could then step down as a full-time Grand Prix driver and concentrate on development and testing. I consider that I could be a good racing driver or a good engineer. I feel that I could be a better racing driver than I am, and I could be a better engineer than I am, but I could be a better engineer than a racing driver, and the company is going to be dependent on its cars and its engineering more than on its drivers in the future.

In the past we have managed to race Can-Am cars in North America one weekend and Grand Prix cars in Europe the next, just by treating each event as another race and not getting carried away by the enormity of the tasks involvement in running two completely different racing teams an ocean apart. When we talked about doing the Indy 500, we said right, let's do it, but let's treat it as just another race. That must have lasted until the car actually started to take shape! Then the enthusiasm for this one race just seemed to snowball. I don't think we were ever as excited about one race before!

We decided that we would make a big effort to win the '500' when we were huddled round a radio listening to the report of the 1969 race. When Denny was lying second with 100 miles to go and then dropped out, we looked at each other and just sort

of decided that we would have to do the job properly for him and build him a car. Denny was ready.

This is one of the things that helps, because Indy is a spooky sort of concrete bowl that demands a special sort of approach. I was a bit sceptical about all the stuff I'd heard about the special requirements for Indianapolis drivers, but a few quick laps round the two-and-a-half-mile oval and you realise it's a pretty special sort of place. Certainly not my ideal track, but special, nevertheless.

We have enjoyed a lot of success in American racing lately but we certainly didn't set sail for Indy thinking we were going to 'do a Can-Am' there. We were all aware that there were a lot of capable people who had been there a long time and knew a hell of a lot more about it than us. We knew we had to go there and learn.

We fitted an Offenhauser engine in preference to the four-cam Indy Ford engine mainly because we thought it was a simpler, cleaner, more reliable, and less thirsty engine than the Ford. It isn't as fast as the Ford, but we'd like to think it will be around at the finish.

Fuel mileage is a big consideration in a flat-out 500-mile race with averages hovering around 165 m.p.h. We figure on doing a lap of the track per gallon of special Gulf 'dope' fuel with a methanol base—that is, two-and-a-half mpg. That sounds like a fairly catastrophic fuel consumption from the turbocharged 'Offy', but it's practically economy run stuff when you think that the Ford only does about one-and-a-half miles to the gallon!

It isn't just the number of fuel stops that matter when you think of fuel consumption. It also goes a long way towards dictating the shape of the car. Our M15 carries 67 gallons of fuel in special Goodyear safety-cell rubber bags. That's nearly twice as much fuel as we carry in our Grand Prix cars!

McLaren Racing is going from strength to strength. We have around 50 on the staff now and we have extended our workshop facilities to take in a 20,000 sq. ft factory in addition to the 10,000 sq. ft factory which we feared would be too big when we first moved to Colnbrook in 1965.

Lotus started off in much the same way as we have done and they now produce various high-performance road cars. We have thought of building a McLaren road car from time to time, but we keep shelving the plans.

We're too heavily committed in three different types of racing at the moment, to start diversifying and building road cars. I like to think that we will put our minds to building the best road car you could imagine when we have built an image through racing. At present when people find out I'm a racing driver, they wonder if I drive a Lotus or a Ferrari.

We'll build a road car when someone asks Jack Brabham if he drives a McLaren—then I just know we'll be established!

24

Businessman Bruce: HRH the Duke of Edinburgh discusses the Trojan-built McLaren cars with Bruce McLaren at the International Racing Car Show in London.

What do you do when you've been on top of the heap and then the world crashes around you? How do you face up to the fact that after thrice being World Champion you can't even finish a race? Australia's Jack Brabham, confronted with the problem, almost decided to quit. He didn't. And, back amongst the leading contenders, is glad of it. But even so, as he recalls here, 1968 was the ...

YEAR OF DECISION

By JACK BRABHAM

FOR me, 1968 was a terrible year. After winning the world championship in 1966 and coming second in 1967 (to Denny Hulme driving one of our team cars) the 1968 season was one of unqualified disaster. After the first world championship round in South Africa, where Jochen Rindt gave us a third place using one of the previous year's engines, we produced a really dismal record with the new twin-cam Repco engine which we had expected to be so much better than the single-cam unit we had used to such good effect in the two years before.

After the South African GP, Jochen and I finished only one race—the German GP, where Jochen was third and I was fifth. Our list of troubles was endless, and at the end of the season I was mortified to find myself second from the bottom of the world championship table.

Frankly, I seriously considered giving up Formula 1 racing. But thinking about it a bit more made me decide to have another go; after all, it wouldn't have looked very good to bow out at the end of such a disastrous year.

Clearly, the answer was to turn for our power to the Ford-Cosworth V8 engine, which had won all but one of the championship races in 1968. Unfortunately, we were rather late making our decision, and so we had to produce a modification of our 1968 design rather than turn out a brand-new 1969 model.

I remember going down to Goodwood to try the first Ford-powered BT26 before it was shipped to South Africa. I knew right away that it was promising. This seemed to be confirmed during practice at Kyalami for the South African GP when I grabbed pole position. That hadn't happened for quite a while! At that time the Grand Prix cars were wearing wings that seemed to grow in size with each race, and reckon my good time at Kyalami was because we had the best wings in the business.

Did I say the best wings? Joke was that both Jacky Ickx, my new team-mate, and myself, had to retire because of wing breakage!

The other important factor at Kyalami was the tyres. I don't think many race spectators realise just how important tyres are in modern Grand Prix racing. They really do make the difference between winning and losing, and if you are behind in tyres then you can't make it up in any other way. There is an exciting technical battle between the tyre companies; for one race one tyre company will have the winner, and the next time will be overtaken by something new from a rival.

Well, at Kyalami we had some really competitive 'boots', probably because we had done our tyre testing at that circuit. Unfortunately, those tyres didn't suit the circuits for the next three Grands Prix, at Barcelona, Monaco and Zandvoort, and it was not until the French GP at Clermont-Ferrand that we started to be competitive again.

There was one exception to this—the *Daily Express* Trophy at Silverstone at the end of March—which I managed to win after a worrying last lap.

The race was run on a rain-sodden track which never dried out completely, and with Goodyear coming up with a splendid wet-weather tyre I led from start to finish. All the same, it was a darned close thing, because on the last lap my engine began to cough and was clearly running short of fuel. Jochen Rindt was chasing me in his Lotus, and though I started that final lap with a 9·5-second lead over him, my fuel-starved engine made me slower and slower, until finally it cut completely on the last corner. I rolled across the line with a dead engine . . . only 2·2 seconds ahead of Jochen!

Anyway, it was encouraging to take the chequered flag again after such a long time, and with Jacky Ickx fourth as well things looked fairly promising.

Then things went badly again, and made me wonder whether I'd been right in opting to carry on with a GP programme. At Barcelona, in the Spanish GP, we had a tyre problem, and an engine problem, and to cap it all Jacky lost time when his rear wing broke. Repairs to my engine cost around £2,400, and our only consolation was sixth place for Jacky.

The Monaco GP was just as bad. Jacky was going quite well, dicing with Piers Courage for second place, until he had his rear suspension break. For me t was quite an experience, that race, because I had a coming-together with John Surtees' BRM just before we went into the famous tunnel.

John had sudden gearbox trouble and, thinking I was still behind him, he pulled over to let me through . . only I was by then almost alongside. Two of our tyres hit together, taking off one of my rear wheels as clean as a whistle, and so I went on through the tunnel on three wheels and with no brakes. When I got into daylight again I had to run the car into the wall to get it stopped before the run down to the chicane. Quite a moment, I assure you.

The Dutch GP at Zandvoort was a slight improvement, but only slightly, with fifth place for Jacky and sixth for me. We both had problems in the race; in my case it was a vicious oversteer that developed when the fuel level got lower, while Jacky had to slack off for the last couple of laps when his fuel pressure dropped.

This wasn't looking much like a victorious comeback, but I thought we would be in with a chance in the next championship round, the French Grand Prix on the fine circuit at Clermont-Ferrand, because we were getting some improved tyres which I thought would perhaps do the trick.

So a few days before the French race I went up to Silverstone to see how good the tyres were . . . with the result that I missed the three next Grands Prix. Something went wrong with the car as I rushed round Club Corner, and I rammed into the bank.

JACK'S
BACK!

Brabham as the fans know him—cornering hard at Monaco. 1969 saw an upsurge in the Australian's fortunes which led the knowing ones to tip him as a good bet to take his third world title in 1970. As No. 1 in his own GP team and a 'works' driver for Matra in sports cars, life can look good in the 40's.

On any other corner on the circuit I'm sure I would have got away with it, but the normal line through Club takes the car within about eight inches of the protective bank, and that wasn't enough room for manoeuvre. Working from the rev-counter reading, I was doing 113 miles an hour half-way through the corner when things went amuck. The car hooked the bank, and was stopped within about 30 yards, so you can imagine the impact. Trouble was, it was right out of sight of the pits, and so no-one knew what had happened.

It was a terrifying time, because my foot was jammed on the throttle and the engine was revving its head off. The instrument panel was a twisted mess so that I couldn't get to the ignition switch, but with some contortions I was able to slip a finger behind the panel and get the motor stopped. By this time the fuel was rushing out from a split tank and there was a big patch all round the corner. If I hadn't managed to stop the engine there's no doubt the car would have gone on fire, because the exhaust pipes would have got red hot.

There was still a serious threat that fire would break out, but I was solidly jammed in the car and couldn't possibly get out. So I had a dilemma— should I press the built-in fire extinguisher and try to prevent a fire, or wait until a fire started and then press the button?

In the end, I pressed the button because I realised I was completely on my own; in fact, it was half an hour before they got me out of the car.

I'm sure I made the right decision in setting off the extinguisher when I did, because if I'd waited then the extinguisher would have put out the fire in the car but wouldn't have been able to stop the petrol burning round the car and this would have spread back.

It was the longest few minutes I've ever known. At one time I thought it was for ever. Anyway, the physical result was a broken left ankle, which had to be screwed together, and which put me out of action until the Italian Grand Prix in September.

So I wasn't even able to watch the French Grand Prix, where Jacky gave a fine performance, dicing for lap after lap with Jean-Pierre Beltoise in his Matra and only losing second place to the French-man on the last lap. By all accounts it was a tremendous battle between the two of them, and we knew then that our new tyres were working well.

Maybe we were getting well into the season, but at least it looked as though we might pick up a win or two. If only I hadn't been out of action, a two-car effort might have paid bigger dividends.

At least I was able to get along to the next two Grands Prix, even though I wasn't taking part. For the British Grand Prix at Silverstone, Ford came to my rescue with an automatic transmission Zodiac, and I was able to drive up there with my damaged left foot resting on a mound of cushions. There we got an even better result, with Jacky taking second place, though that a close thing. Just before the end, Jacky thought his car was running out of fuel, because it was coughing. In fact, there were still a few gallons left at the end of the race, and the stuttering of the engine was probably due to it getting a gulp of air in the fuel system.

Anyway, the engine stopped on the last lap, and it seems Jacky thought it was out of petrol and so didn't try to restart it. He coasted a lot of the way home, getting slower and slower, and rolled across the line with a dead engine with Bruce McLaren storming up behind him. He got that second place by just a few seconds. It was murder being in the pits and watching it happen. How I wish I could have been in a car at that time on the circuit instead of worrying about Jacky!

However, it was more than encouraging, and with a second place under the team's belt we thought it was about time we had a victory. And Jacky gave us just that in the German Grand Prix at Nürburgring, where he really dominated the race. It was a tremendous, quite fantastic performance. He really drove brilliantly.

The Nürburgring, with its 170-corners and a lap of over 14 miles, is a real test of driving ability and one place where experience of the circuit pays dividends. Jacky has done a lot of driving around the 'Ring—he thinks more than 10,000 miles—and I was confident before the race that he would do well.

That day at Nürburgring at the beginning of August, Jacky was right on top. The car was right and he was just in the right frame of mind. Above all, the tyres were good. Before the race a motoring journalist asked me how I thought Jacky would go, and for once I was full of confidence, for I not only felt he would go well but also that the BT26 would stand up to the punishment. The Nürburgring has a number of points where the cars take off completely —all four wheels—and this puts a tremendous strain on the suspension, but I thought we had a car strong enough to take any amount of that sort of punishment.

It was a great moment for me when Jacky crossed the line in first place, well ahead of the rest of the field. It had been just under two years since one of my cars had won a major classic—the Canadian Grand Prix at Mosport in 1967—and my only regret was that we had a second car sitting in the paddock at the 'Ring with no-one to drive it.

For the Italian Grand Prix at Monza I was back in business. Walking on my damaged left ankle wasn't very funny, but it was sufficiently recovered to allow me to operate the clutch, and I was determined to have a go. In fact, as it turned out, it was a disastrous week, for we blew up two engines during practice in England, blew up two more during official practice at Monza, and had to borrow an engine from Frank Williams in order to get Jacky to the start of the race. (The cheapest blow-up of that quartet came to about £800, so you can see what I mean by disastrous!)

The race wasn't any better, either. I only lasted a few laps before I had a fuel line break, while Jacky ran into trouble and failed to finish.

Was the German result a flash in the pan? I didn't think so, and remembering that our cars had scored a one-two in the Canadian Grand Prix two years earlier, I thought we might do well again at Mosport.

Practice didn't look very hopeful, because we had an engine go, and then we had another one turn sick during the shakedown practice on race morning. The mechanics had changed the first engine in about two and a quarter hours, and they did the second switch in under two hours. And I was glad they did, because Jacky got his second GP win of the season, and I was second.

By now, Jacky was in with an outside chance of ousting Jackie Stewart for the championship; it was only a slight possibility, but it was still there. But in the United States Grand Prix, at Watkins Glen, Jacky had engine failure at three-quarter distance, and I had to be content with fourth place after making a stop to take on more fuel with 15 laps to go. I had been sniffing petrol fumes for some time, and suspected an empty front tank, but in fact the trouble was that the fuel wasn't picking up to get to the engine. This cost me one place, because I was overtaken by John Surtees in his BRM.

For much of the race, though, Jacky and I had been dicing with Piers Courage for second place. Piers was driving a BT26, and he really had a go that day; for some reason I wasn't getting enough revs along the straight, and since this was the only possible overtaking section I just couldn't take him.

So to the final round, 7,000 feet above sea level at Mexico City, where Jacky and I found our tyres well suited to the circuit. I got pole position by a margin of more than half a second, and Jacky was on the front row beside me.

In the race, my former team-mate, Denny Hulme, drove very well indeed in his McLaren and got the chequered flag. My engine went rather off-song, and the terrific heat affected Jacky, who felt very unwell for a while but then recovered to give Denny a terrific battle towards the finish, losing out by only some two and a half seconds.

So it was second and third for our team. Jacky had finished second in the drivers' world championship and we were also second in the Formula 1 manufacturers' championship.

Maybe we hadn't done quite as well as we had expected after that practice showing at the beginning of the season in South Africa, but the team had a couple of victories to show for the effort, three second places, two thirds a fifth and two sixths. With cars that were basically a year old at the start of the season in terms of design that wasn't too bad, I suppose.

Anyway, it was good enough to make me feel I'd done the right thing in deciding to stay in Grand Prix racing, and it encouraged me to continue in 1970.

THE RISE OF

MARCH

Eoin Young

HISTORICALLY speaking, I don't think it's ever happened before. And it probably won't happen again. It was almost unbelievable that Jackie Stewart, the new World Champion, and a canny Scot if ever there was one, should sign to drive a car that only existed on a drawing board! It would take an audacious organisation to even suggest that the world champion might like to drive their car, but I suppose audacity is one of the strong points of March Engineering. It never occurred to them when they were sitting down and planning the basis of their operation back in March 1969 that they could fail. They had even taken into account while Jackie Stewart was winning the first of his championship GPs, that by the end of the season Matra might not be requiring his services. Here, they thought, was the ideal customer for their new car, because it would be so difficult for a private entrant to buy a competitive car anywhere else for a driver as fast as Stewart.

March Engineering is basically four men, and their initials help to form the title of the company. M is for Max Mosley, sometime racer, ex-barrister and currently an extremely polished public relations man and sponsor-getter. Mosley must have tracked down a cool £100,000 to start the company before the world at large even knew of their plans! Rumours of the identity of the phantom sponsors who had asked to remain anonymous, included the Ministry of Technology, Guinness' stout, a biscuit company, the Ford Motor Company and Firestone tyres. A man with bar training like Mosley could

charm the birds from the trees, and he had done a lot to make the motor racing 'establishment' respect the name of the fledgling company even before a car appeared.

The A was really thrown in to make up the word, but it could stand for Alan Rees, another ex-racer of some note, who distinguished himself by running the super-successful Winkelmann Racing Team in Formula 2. The team was noted for its high standard of preparation and organisation and Rees manages the new March team, with a lot of help from another ex-Winkelmann man, Peter Kerr who moved to March as chief mechanic/engineer.

C is for Graham Coaker, the oldest of the four at 37, who left Hawker Siddeley to set up a production line of racing cars for March. Coaker is probably the least known of the March men, but he is working to put that right. He has had a lot of experience in Formula 3 cars and knows what the customers require.

The H is probably the most important letter, as it stands for Herd, Robin Herd, the designer who gave up drawing fragments of the Concorde at the Royal Aircraft Establishment to join the growing McLaren team and learn the skilled art of designing successful racing cars. He found that the more complicated and tricky bits usually don't work in a racing car. They look fine as a design idea on a piece of paper, but they complicate the car. And successful cars are invariably simple, straightforward, reliable and fast.

He went from McLaren to Cosworth where he

Driver's-eye-view of the March racing car which made its Grand Prix début in 1970 (opposite) and (above) much-travelled New Zealand auto reporter, Eoin Young, author of this article.

In the winter sunshine of Silverstone in February, the March Formula 1 car is unveiled for the benefit of reporters, photographers and television. World Champion Jackie Stewart (above) takes a blue-painted March to be raced by the Ken Tyrrell Organisation, through Woodcote Corner; and (below) on the same corner, Chris Amon drives the red-painted March which, sponsored by the American STP Corporation, is one of the official works team cars. French ace, Johnny Servoz-Gavin, is No. 2 to Stewart in the Tyrrell team while Jo Siffert, of Switzerland, is Chris Amon's team-mate. STP are also running a third car with American star, Mario Andretti, at the wheel. A few weeks after their first public appearance, the March cars lined up for the South African Grand Prix with both Stewart and Amon on the front row, Stewart eventually finishing third.

designed the still-born four-wheel drive chassis to take Keith Duckworth's special transmission. It was a good car, but it never raced. The problem lay in the fact that the general concept of four-wheel-drive on its original forms had been a failure for Cosworth as well as Matra, Lotus and McLaren.

It was Herd's reputation as a designer that tempted Jackie Stewart, Chris Amon and Jo Siffert to gamble with a valuable year of their careers. They signed to drive a car that didn't exist, believing that Herd's ability could almost guarantee them a winner.

The idea of building their own racing car really started for Herd and Rees when they were at school together, sitting in the back row of the divinity class reading Denis Jenkinson's Grand Prix reports in *Motor Sport*. Later Herd met Mosley at Oxford when they were both doing Physics. Herd collected double firsts in Physics and Engineering while Mosley switched to law and went on to be a barrister before the racing bug bit.

Secrecy was imperative in the early stages of their plans since each was working at other jobs, and if the plans fell through they would tell nobody and the world would never know of their ambitions. But when all the parts fell into place and they secured the lease on very attractive factory premises just outside Bicester, near Oxford, they announced their existence and set up shop with a handful of helpers in what looked like a big bare workshop. Within weeks the staff and production had expanded into the building next door, as the motoring press clamoured for more details of the new March cars.

They had hoped to secure the driving services of either Jochen Rindt or Chris Amon. Rindt and Rees had come close to building a car of their own a year earlier, and Herd had worked closely with Chris Amon when the New Zealander was driving for the McLaren team before he joined Ferrari. Plans were so far ahead that Herd was able to mention the possibility of a 1970 drive to Amon at the Spanish Grand Prix in Barcelona in May, 1969. Rindt cemented a favourable contract with Lotus late in the year, but Amon had been getting more and more unhappy with his lot at Ferrari and after a confused series of contract making and breaking fanned by

a hostile Italian press, Chris thought he would join the new March team.

Strong rumour suggested that Ken Tyrrell would in fact order March cars for Jackie Stewart, and eventually he did, but before this he had made advances to BRM to get monocoques specially built for him to take the Ford engine. His advances were

ppy Ken Tyrrell, standing in the back of his own porter, discusses the technicalities of racing tyres with nlop expert.

35

turned down, and Ken placed his order with March. They guaranteed him delivery by the first day of February, but Tyrrell, with years of hearing such promises on delivery which were always broken, openly doubted their ability to meet the delivery date.

They were so sure of their production men, that they suggested Ken might like to place the purchase price of the car—£9,000—on the line for a double-or-quits bet. If they didn't have the car ready by February 1st, Ken would have the car for nothing. If they did meet the deadline, Ken's first car for Jackie would set him back £18,000! The bet wasn't taken, but as from then Ken must have felt a little better about his chances of early delivery. . . .

There are no tricky features about the Grand Prix car. 'It's tolerably conventional; something that we know can finish races,' says designer Herd. Departures from standard practice appear in the cast magnesium front bulkhead. In most racing cars these bulkheads which brace the aluminium sheet of the monocoque, are fabricated from steel. Another Herd idea is to divide the normal rubber fuel bag which runs down each side of the monocoque beside the driver, into three separate fuel cells on each side. Herd maintains that this will ensure an even ride height as the fuel load drops during the race.

Keeping the car simple, the front suspension is mounted outboard. So are the disc brakes. They will use 13-inch wheels all round to begin with.

Their first project was to design and build a prototype Formula 3 car to see whether their talents

37

The power-house: the Ford-Cosworth engine which makes the March car tick (left) and (above) Chris Amon pulls in after a trial run.

Tyre technicians, engine designer, mechanics, team manager and many others are needed before Jackie Stewart and Johnny Servoz-Gavin take to the track in their March cars.

were capable of combining. The car took shape in secret, and when Allan Rollinson ran it for the first time at Silverstone it clipped a second off the lap record! From then on all systems were GO.

The essence of March is the combination of talent. Each man is in command of his own area. Herd is regarded as very much the man to talk to with regard to design and development, but as soon as the car reaches the track, the man who looks after things is Alan Rees. The same goes for Mosley and Coaker who was the anchor man as the factory gradually gathered pace for full production.

It was Coaker who arranged for the local council to visit the factory and be impressed by the sincerity and real efforts the small group was making. The councillors left with the definite impression that March might put Bicester on the map despite the worries of one that the pleasant little Bucks village might change overnight to a grimy motor town like Coventry or Cowley! It was Coaker who hounded the telephone department until they provided lines for the new company.

If you look back in racing history you will find that Raymond Mays, now 71 and still with the BRM team he founded, did a March-like operation back in 1934. He built the ERA in a tin shed at Bourne with co-operation from Peter Berthon, Reid Railton, Humphry Cook, and engine-man Murray Jamieson. The war saw the end of the ERA as a force in British racing, but Mays had soon gathered enthusiasm to start off the BRM project and by 1951 they were fielding the superb-sounding controversial, seldom-successful, $1\frac{1}{2}$-litre V16 supercharged cars.

A similar sort of project might have happened in racing history, but never before has there been a brand new team suddenly formed with a brand new car to challenge the best Grand Prix cars in the world on an equal footing. It's a little bit like walking in off the street and asking the army recruiting officer if they have any vacancies for generals.

If audacity coupled with ability can produce an 'instant' Grand Prix car that works, the men of March will write themselves straight into the history books!

SO YOU WANT TO BE A RACING DRIVER?

asks Ron Naylor

Some tips from the instructor for the author as he takes his place in a single-seat racing car for the very first time.

COURAGE, according to some experts, is no longer considered a vital factor in a racing driver's make-up. In the past decade the sport has become more and more a science needing a scientific approach to building racing cars and driving them.

Gone are the ruddy-faced young drivers who raced mainly for honour and glory. To these young men motor racing seemed a noble sport and the 'pukka thing to do' as they sped round the race tracks with bare arms showing below short-sleeved sports shirts. The only piece of protective equipment they wore was . . . a crash helmet and sometimes not even that.

But today their place in the modern compact single seater has been taken by skilful technicians who wear protective clothing from head to foot. For the present day racing driver to do well in this razor-edged business, it is vital he knows every nut and bolt in the car he is driving, diagnose on the spot every little noise that may develop during a race; under-

stand, interpret and obey the mechanics instructions, and then throw in two very important ingredients of his own—aggressiveness and competitiveness.

Motor racing, though, is still a challenge and an exciting 'occupation' or sport. But with speeds continuing to increase on racing circuits throughout the world, it is becoming more and more important that drivers get proper training at an early stage.

Seeing young drivers competing in club events doing all the wrong things and spinning off the track in a frightening manner, makes supporters of motor racing wish something more could be done to train them.

In this country there are two schools already set up and well established. They are the Jim Russell School, which operates at Snetterton, and the Motor Racing Stables who have training centres at Brands Hatch, Silverstone and Mallory Park race circuits.

Both schools have expert instructors willing and

Ron Naylor amongst some young (and some not-so-young) hopefuls in the classroom of Motor Racing Stables school for drivers at Brands Hatch.

Blackboard tuition comes first before pupils are allowed to take a car on to the circuit. An instructor goes through the basic rules here—including the various flag signals used to warn drivers.

Then, before taking his pupil out in a saloon car, the instructor outlines the circuit and indicates the corners and other spots where special attention is needed.

eager to pass on the experience and knowledge they have gained on the race track. Between them, the marshals and mechanics, all of whom help to guide the young pupils, they have a pretty good record on the safety front and have brought along a whole host of really professional drivers.

But many more potentially good drivers have fallen by the wayside, forced to drop out of the training courses through lack of funds.

Geoffrey Clarke, managing director of Motor Racing Stables, estimates that some 2,000 young drivers start training at the Brands Hatch 'stable' in Kent every year but less than 20 per cent are able to continue and finish the course. Despite the school having introduced a system of 'pay-as-you-learn', the vast majority of the pupils are defeated by costs which amount to about £100 spread over a period which could vary considerably depending on ability and time available. All too often, though, pupils run out of money not time and are unable to assess their true ability as racing drivers.

While the school makes every effort not to lose potentially good driver material, it is also considered equally important for a newcomer to discover at the very outset whether he is any good and has a chance of making the grade.

For this reason the instructors carry out a very careful and thorough analysis of each pupil's driving ability by accompanying them on three laps of the circuit in a saloon car. They look for smoothness in driving and calmness in the driver, hurried or jerky movements, gear changing or braking on bends, or when the front wheels are at an angle, are all considered bad faults. While many drivers get away with these bad habits on the road, they would be less fortunate on the race circuit.

Points are deducted for faulty driving—the number of points varies according to the seriousness of the fault. If a pupil returns less than 60 points, though, he is a non-starter for a training course.

Obviously it is better for pupils to find out their shortcomings this way than by discovering them during a race when they can be a danger to themselves and other competitors.

Next stage in the course is the 'briefing'. Here pupils' faults undergo a further analysis, and instruc-

tion is given on the rule of the track, flag signals and on the line to steer through a bend. Then comes the first drive in a single-seater.

Changing from a saloon car to a single-seater is like hopping off a cart horse and mounting a racehorse. By comparison a saloon car is slow to respond and leaves time in hand to correct most mistakes. A single-seater, on the other hand, will dart off in all sorts of directions if the driver gets 'all crossed up'.

My first drive in a single-seater racing car—a Formula Ford—consisted of five laps of the 1·24-mile circuit at Brands Hatch. It was an exhilarating experience and like most newcomers to single-seaters I had to fight against apprehension.

The instructor's advice was helpful. 'Forget it is a single-seater,' he said. 'Forget it is Brands Hatch racing circuit, forget you are wearing a crash helmet, just treat it as another piece of road and another car. Go out and enjoy the experience.' So I did. But it

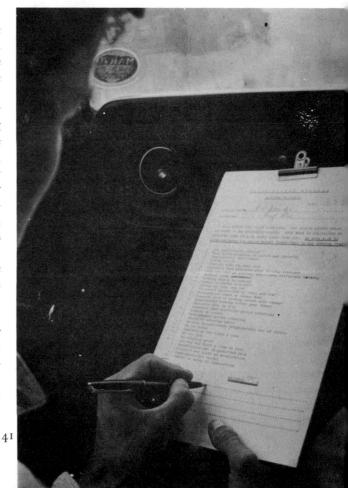

The novice's first experience of the race circuit comes at the wheel of a saloon car before he is allowed to tackle the real thing. During this preliminary trial, the instructor not only assesses the potential of the candidate but also takes the opportunity to brief him on the correct driving techniques at each part of the circuit. It looks as if pupil Naylor took a wrong turning here.

took a little time and a few laps to forget all the points he mentioned.

Having got the feel of the car, I was pleasantly surprised—and reassured—at the way it hugged the track and changed direction at the slightest touch of the steering wheel.

The 'briefing session' proved extremely useful. I quickly found I could aim the car to within an inch or two of any corner; the controls were positive and although I could not see the foot pedals, even when I peered inside the car, they were easy to find—easier still in stockinged feet. Once I got used to driving the car lying almost flat on my back, I soon began to feel part of it and started to do as the instructor suggested: 'Enjoy the experience'. The old adage of driving a car through the seat of your pants began to have some meaning.

My performance during the five exploratory laps was well received and I moved to the next stage—personal instruction. Here the points made at the 'briefing' were demonstrated, first with the instructor at the wheel of a saloon car and myself watching his every move from the passenger seat, and then with positions reversed.

Back in the single-seater apprehension was replaced by a tenseness, a feeling I recognised from race days in other sports. Yet the odd thing was—this was no race. Nevertheless I became tight in the stomach and as I headed for the notorious Paddock Bend the feeling got worse. I knew the instructor was watching my every move and I wanted to do well—a natural competitive spirit.

Paddock Bend is one of the most difficult bends on British motor racing circuits. On the approach to the

42

Ron Naylor leaves the pits at Brands Hatch for his first drive in a single-seater. Behind, another pupil in a saloon car waits anxiously as the instructor checks on his grading sheet before deciding whether or not it is worthwhile for the novice to continue with his lessons. Only about 20 per cent of the hopefuls go on to complete the course.

Bend there is a slight hump, which has been the undoing of many young drivers trying too hard, then the track sweeps down and away to the right limiting the driver's vision ahead.

As I headed for the Bend, the hump looked more like a hill from such a low position. But once over the hump, I began looking for the first marker—a white line on the left hand side of the track.

I was almost on it before I spotted it, and was just about to stand hard on the brakes when I remembered my instructor's advice.

'A quick stab on the brakes, then put the wheel hard over, aiming to clip the grass on the inside of the track as close as possible at the apex, thus taking a straight line through the bend.

'Now let the car drift over to the extreme left hand side of the track and on with the power. Up the hill,

and just past the bridge heel-toe change down into third. Hold the car steady on a straight course heading for the next marker—an advertising sign—then a full right lock with a bit of power to take you through Druids Hill Bend—a tight hairpin.

'Don't drift too far to the left, keep as near to the centre as possible and steer for the right hand side of the track. Straighten up and on with the power, changing up into top gear. The advertising sign directly ahead is the next marker, so continue building up speed and when in line with the sign, turn the wheel hard left taking a straight line through a wide left hander into the Bottom Straight, powering all the time.'

Holding the wheel steady and feeling the wind rushing past my cheeks, I remembered that this was the second fastest section of track on the 'Brands'

43

short circuit and it was here that some valuable seconds could be gained. So I kept the power on.

Again I recalled the instructor's words.

'Keep over to the right. Check rear-view mirror for anyone who may be trying to overtake. A quick glance and then start looking for the next turning point—a white line on the side of the track. Stab the brakes and as the front wheels hit the marker line, wheel over to the left. Clip the grass and let the car drift over to the right to clip the next corner. A little more power and steer straight for the centre of the big advertising sign ahead. Just before you run off the track, brake hard, off the pedal and steer hard right.'

I remembered that this was perhaps the most difficult manoeuvre on the track. I was heading for Clearways and if I deviated a little either way, or applied too much power I could spin off.

But the advice of the expert returned.

'Keep to the centre of the circuit until clear of the Pits entrance and then put the wheel over to steer to the right. You should now be lined up for the Top Straight and be aiming directly for the Paddock Bend turning point ready for the next lap.' And I was.

This is the fastest section of the short circuit and it is here pupils get their first real sensation of speed as they sweep past the Pits and the Grandstand.

The course calls for a further nine laps—all untimed and without incident—before the single-seater test in Class 6 is completed and throughout the ten laps a close eye must be kept on the rev counter to ensure the specified 4,500 revs limit is not exceeded.

Success in this test leads to automatic up-grading to Class 5 in which the timed laps begin with increased revs limit of not more than 5,000. To reach Class 4 a lap time of 74 seconds for four consecutive laps must be returned, which is a little more difficult than some pupils imagine.

From then on it is basically a question of practice and more practice with a few more tests thrown in.

Class 4 is divided into five stages—improved lap times, further tests with an instructor, ten laps in wet weather, special training session on a skid pan, and a written paper on flag signals and race procedure.

Lap times must again be improved to reach Class 2 together with a total of 12 laps with times of within

COST OF MOTOR RACING TUITION

	£	s	d
Initial trial and analysis	10	10	0
Personal instruction	5	5	0
Membership of Motor Racing Stable			
* Club & Racing School*	5	0	0
10 laps in Class 6 (untimed)	10	0	0
10 laps in Class 5 (timed)	10	0	0
10 laps in Class 4 (timed)	10	0	0
Skid pan instruction	5	5	0
Class 3 test	3	3	0
10 laps in Class 3	10	0	0
(Qualifying for Class 2 Test)			
* 12 laps Class 2 Test*	12	0	0
	£81	3	0

As nobody has yet qualified from each class in the minimum number of laps it is more realistic to budget for a minimum of £100.

approximately one second of the time set by the instructor in the same car on the same day.

Drivers reaching Class 2 grade can compete in single-seater races in public and upgrading to Class 1 depends on performance and race results. Those who reach the top class qualify for sponsored races or may be offered a management contract in which racing costs are subsidised by the training school.

The instructors' motto at Brands Hatch stable is: 'catch 'em young', for drivers are then easily moulded. Enthusiasts aged 12 and 13 years have attended the 'stable' seeking instruction and many have shown considerable flair.

One success story frequently quoted at the Motor Racing Stable centres is that of a 17-year-old who took the course before passing his Ministry of Transport driving test. He took the test on the Monday following his 17th birthday and won his first single-seater race the next week-end.

And finally the moment every aspiring racing-driver has been waiting for. Ron Naylor (above) in full flight—at the wheel of racing car at last—and who knows what Walter Mitty-like dreams of being Stirling Moss are going through his head. But there's always a warning to bring up the reckless with a start (on right).

NOTICE
WARNING TO THE PUBLIC
MOTOR RACING IS
DANGEROUS

"IT IS A CONDITION OF ADMISSION THAT ALL PERSONS HAVING ANY CONNECTION WITH THE PROMOTION AND/OR ORGANISATION AND/OR CONDUCT OF THE MEETING, INCLUDING THE OWNERS OF THE LAND AND THE DRIVERS AND OWNERS OF THE VEHICLES AND PASSENGERS IN THE VEHICLES ARE ABSOLVED FROM ALL LIABILITY ARISING OUT OF ACCIDENT CAUSING DAMAGE OR PERSONAL INJURY (WHETHER FATAL OR OTHERWISE) HOWSOEVER CAUSED TO SPECTATORS OR TICKET HOLDERS"

Sunday Mirror columnist Mark Kahn struck a blow for every middle-aged suburban husband when he broke into international rallying at an age when most are looking for armchair and slippers. He chose to start at the top —with the Monte and RAC Rallies. After all, says Mark, he had left it a bit late to begin at the bottom.

from TUBBY HUBBY to RALLY DRIVER

Mark Kahn

WHAT happens to the youthful would-be racing or rally driver in his sports car? It is a highly pertinent question in considering the Kahn international rallying career.

The easy answer is that he grows up (if he does not kill himself first), acquires a family, a family car, a paunch, and the staidness that comes with 45 or 50 years.

But it is my firmly-held belief that sometimes a chubby hubby is driving home to suburbia from the office in his dull saloon, a gleam comes into his eye, his hands grasp the wide, wide wheel more firmly, his arms straighten. Then his right foot moves in a heel-and-toe parody (if he hasn't sunk to automatic transmission) and, snick, down he goes into third.

With his foot down he goes into the corner. A touch of the opposites. And suddenly the city road has changed into an icy Alpine col. It is a bleak snowy night, and he is hard on Hopkirk's heels . . .

That Demon Boy has emerged from the depths of years of repression and taken control. Fortunately for our Walter Mitty and those around him, the

46

phantom is banished in a flash back to the unconscious.

And even if you, sir, deny ever having been a boy racer, I am willing to bet a set of racing tyres to a spark plug that you, too, have had your moments, moments when you have thought that if Carlsson could do it, why not you? If only you had the car, the opportunity.

All of which will explain why it suddenly occurred to me—a middle-aged (but youthful middle-aged, if you understand me) and overweight man—to say to the Editor of the *Sunday Mirror*: 'Why don't you let me enter the Monte Carlo Rally and write about it in the paper? After all, if a works driver does it, well, that's his job. If *I* finish, it's a story.'

And that was how I found myself on the Monte in 1967 with Tommy Wisdom and Peter Jopp.

It was a late entry, and so we had to start from Reims instead of with the other British at Dover. But the rally really started for me at Tulse Hill in South London.

It was Thursday morning, two days before the start. We had collected our Cortina GT from where it had been prepared near Olympia, and were on our way to Lydd Airfield, Kent. Our plan was to fly the car to Le Touquet, have a leisurely lunch there (I'm very good at leisurely lunches) and then drive down to Reims, getting the feel of the car on the way. Scrutineering Friday. Off Saturday. Bob would be our uncle.

But it was in South London that Wisdom (or it might have been Jopp) said casually to me: 'You have your licence, of course?' 'My international competition licence? Of course,' I replied a trifle stiffly. Did they take me for a fool? 'No, no,' said Jopp (or it might have been Wisdom) 'Your ordinary, British driving licence. The scrutineers will want to see it.'

My ordinary British driving licence. Have you ever suddenly gone cold all over? They stopped the car while I searched frantically. Then, 'No,' I said. 'I haven't got my ordinary British driving licence.'

'Phone home and ask someone to rush it down here.'

'There won't be anyone home,' I said, 'until tonight.'

'I suppose you *have* got a licence,' said Wisdom gently (I'm sure *that* was Wisdom) 'I mean, they haven't taken it away from you?'

I exploded at him. When I had finished they took me to Tulse Hill station. 'You'll just have to go home and get it,' they said. 'Join us at Reims.'

Courteously they waved goodbye. It said *Frequent electric trains to London* at the station entrance. I waited, it seemed, half a day before one turned up. And here I have some advice. If you ever want to go to Palmers Green, North London, where I live, don't start from Tulse Hill.

The train took me to London Bridge. I felt that a taxi home from there would take too long through the London traffic. The tube to Wood Green, my nearest station, I thought, and *then* a taxi to Palmers Green. There aren't, I discovered, any taxis at Wood Green. So it had to be a long, trundling bus ride. Then a ten-minute half-walk-half-run to home.

I dashed in. The Kahn Labrador didn't even wake up. What a guard dog, I thought savagely, and made a note to have him destroyed when the rally was over.

By some miracle I laid my hands on the licence (I can never find it, usually). That half-walk-half-run lark again. Another bus ride. At Wood Green I took the tube to the Air Terminal in the Cromwell Road and got a ticket for the first plane to Paris. At Le Bourget I got a car to the Gare de l'ouest. The driver must have seen me coming. He charged about five quid. And there I got the train for Reims.

I settled back wondering what sort of lunch Wisdom and Jopp were having. A familiar voice said: 'What the hell are you doing here?' It was photographer Frank Charman, sent to cover our departure. I told him the story and swore him to secrecy. I had never seen Charman laugh before.

The unkindest cut happened at Reims station. I hailed a cab. 'Lion d'Or Hotel,' I said, 'sil vous plait.' The driver burst into a torrent of quickfire colloquial French. You know how they do. I had gone through too much to cope with that. 'Lion d'Or,' I said firmly and sprang in with Charman. The driver looked at us, shrugged, and drove us about 100 yards to the Lion d'Or. It cost seven francs. Well, how was I to know it was only 100 yards from the station?

Anyway I arrived there before Wisdom and Jopp. I suspect to this day that they had eaten lunch twice.

After scrutineering, Jopp (or it might have been Wisdom) said to me: 'It is a tradition of the Monte that the cars start gleaming. You are the junior member of this crew. You are elected to clean the car.' 'You are mad,' I said. 'I never clean my own car (all who know me will bear witness to this) and I am not going to clean this one.'

I had no objection, however to taking it down the road to a garage and letting them clean it. Price: 24 francs. The good Frenchmen were hard at work when another rally car pulled in. It was covered in dirt. Two women got out. They looked around and saw the Cortina with its rally plates, then spotted me.

One strode purposefully over. 'Mr Kahn?' I admitted it. 'We wish we could have our car cleaned.'

'Why not?' I said. 'When they've finished mine.' I added: '24 francs.'

'But we can't spare 24 francs from our budget.'

She looked at me. Kahns are nothing if not chivalrous. I reached for my wallet, took out 30 francs. 'Have this one on me,' I said, 'and give 'em a tip.'

The lady took the money. She said with deep gratitude: 'I shall write and thank your Editor.'

'No!' I almost screamed. I wasn't supposed to spend the firm's money like that.

The rally? Oh, that was all right. We finished with only a few moments of drama. One was when I discovered that a cache of pills I have to take had almost vanished. Jopp had eaten them. 'I like the peppermint flavour,' he explained. I waited for him to die in agony. But nothing happened. The other

moment was when Wisdom lost his monocle under the seat. That nearly put us out. We found it just in time.

And so to the RAC Rally of 1968. I embarked on this with my friend John Miles, TV's famous Master Driver and the man who runs the British School of Motoring's High Performance Course.

We had met while I was doing the course, although I never got one of the gold medals which Mr Miles awards to those he considers have carried out a faultless test drive. We got on tolerably well, and besides, I thought it would be nice to have someone a lot older than myself in the car. At any rate, he looked a lot older!

Anyway, we set off full of fight and confidence in one of BSM chairman Denise McCann's Cortina GTs.

The first special stages on the Forestry Commission's land were a hideous revelation. Never had I seen so many potholes, so much rubble. And I didn't like the look of the trees either. The car leap-

ing like a bucking broncho. Our helmeted heads hitting the roof. Arms going like fiddlers' elbows. Opposite-locking, correcting, sliding, slithering. Idiotic spectators running across our path. *What the hell was I doing here?*

A couple more stages and the Halda, which gives exact measurement of distances, ceased to function. I tried hitting it, but it was stubborn, so I had a go at its interior. Have you ever tried to repair a Halda in a rally car that is in turbulent motion?

With a mechanical genius I had never until that moment realised I possessed, I got it going again.

I looked up triumphantly—to find the car gyrating. It spun, lurched, and stopped with its nose in between the posts of a gateway through which, as it happened, we were supposed to go. 'Look at that,' said Mr Miles proudly, 'judged to a T.' John, if I may continue in public the long argument we have had in private over this episode, I have never seen anything so lucky in my puff.

More stages. The Halda fell to pieces. Mr Miles

In the Centre Airport Hotel restaurant, Mark explains how easy this rally business is to the amusement of Jean Barratt, motoring editor of Woman. Co-driver John Miles just looks disbelieving.

was scrabbling on the floor trying to find some of the bits. I had got my foot well buried on the throttle. A sharp left turn downhill. The car didn't respond to the wheel.

We did a sort of motor-cycle wall of death ride round a high embankment. The startled Miles looked up, peered through the windscreen and instead of road, saw branches and sky. The car drifted to the other side of the road and came to a definite stop.

Miss McCann's pretty Cortina was not so pretty. The front wheels were splayed at extraordinary

Another journalist, Hamish Cardno, of Motor, with Doug Lockyer in a Saab on the 1968 RAC International Rally of Great Britain.

angles. The front suspension was, if I may quote Sean O'Casey, 'in a terrible state of chassis.'

The rally had finished for us. We stood there on a deserted road in darkest Somerset—and nothing can be darker than Somerset in those circumstances—and surveyed the wreck of the car and the wreck of our hopes. We felt, suddenly, very tired and cold and hungry and sad.

It was at this moment that a thought occurred to me.

I tapped Miles on the shoulder. 'Does this mean,' I asked, 'that I don't get my gold medal?'

I refuse to print his reply.

To those considering having a go at a rally, I can give only this advice: try to keep the car in one piece. It is humiliating to travel home by train.

I brooded on this reverse for a year. Which brought John Miles and myself to the 1969 RAC Rally. Note the courage of Mr Miles. He didn't turn a hair when I put it to him that we ought to do this rally again.

This time the car was the Kahn Mini-Cooper 1275S. I had been maintaining for a year that I would have got through that bend (which Miles christened Kahn's Corner) in my mini whatever happened to the front suspension.

I was looking forward to that, but the rally organisers, clearly not wishing to put me through that particular test again, had re-routed the whole thing so that we went in the reverse direction. Kind of them, really.

With wheels and tyres scrounged from the munificent Julian Bell and Jeremy Ferguson of Dunlop, a Halda borrowed from British Leyland's long-suffering competitions manager, Peter Browning, and an imposing array of lights from Lucas, we set off, as they say, in good nick.

And this time I greeted the special stages, pot-holes, trees and all, like old friends. I must say, however, that whoever put the logs in the middle of some of the tracks has a lot to answer for.

We were enjoying ourselves. As our heads hit the roof once I remember remarking to John Miles: 'We have our ups and downs.' A little humour does no harm, does it John?

We were doing fine. Even when we hit ice. One stage was a bit hairy for John who was driving, because his door kept flying open, and he had to hold it shut, steer and change gear all at the same time—which he did with considerable aplomb. He grumbled a bit, mind you.

Another moment came half way along a stage when Mr Miles, still driving, rapped my knee. 'Take your foot off the clutch!' he yelled.

'You've gone raving mad!' I screamed back. 'My foot's nowhere near the clutch.'

'Something is!' he yelled.

We looked down. The heater had fallen on to the clutch. We tied it up on the run and carried on.

'I thought you were playing footsie,' said Mr Miles.

But now the lights were failing. Waiting our turn at the next stage we switched the engine off. There wasn't enough juice in the battery to start again on the switch. We had to push-start the car.

We had just started the penultimate of the stages we were to do when the snow came down—hard. The leaders were lucky; they got through the stage with no trouble. But for us, way back at Number 107, it was tough going. The snow came down with blizzard-like intensity. The headlights had gone. Only the spotlights were working faintly.

We pressed on, hardly able to see more than a few feet ahead. If we could have seen how high up we were and the sheer drops, we would have been tempted to call it a night there and then.

Spiked tyres would have helped, but they aren't allowed in the RAC Rally. I have read that this is because the Forestry Commission feels studs would damage their roads. Damage *those* God-forsaken ruts? They've got to be joking.

We stopped eventually in the snow (outside a cemetery as a melancholy backcloth for the scene), near Chollerford. There wasn't enough in the battery to provide the vestige of a spark. We had had it. But it wasn't our fault this time. An on-the-blink headlight switch had drained the current.

What the hell, I wondered, gloomily contemplating the graves, am I doing here?

The answer is that in some perverted way I like it. So here's to the next RAC Rally (if you'll chance it again, John?)

Al Bochroch's American Merry Go Round

FOLLOWING the Sears Point Trans-Am, in which Mark Donohue's Camaro clinched Chevrolet's second 'Pony Car' championship your American correspondent had dinner with Jim Crow, editor of Road & Track, America's leading motor racing magazine.

Over coffee and Grand Marnier my distinguished companion suggested I list America's ten best road racing drivers. The 'road racing' qualification is significant as so few USAC (Indy car) and almost no NASCAR (stock car) drivers venture beyond their oval track bailiwicks, although the better road racers make frequent USAC excursions.

My top ten were—(1) **Mario Andretti**, (2) **Dan Gurney**, (3) **Parnelli Jones**, (4) **Mark Donohue**, (5) **George Follmer**, (6) **Peter Revson**, (7) **Ronnie Bucknum**, (8) **Chuck Parsons**, (9) **Sam Posey**, (10) **John Cannon**.

Surprisingly the names I jotted on the back of our menu turned out to be almost identical to Jim's own.

We had minor differences. The editor thought John Cannon and Jerry Titus belonged ahead of Parsons and Posey. How to handle A. J. Foyt was a problem. Although Super-Tex and Dan Gurney

Mario Andretti in thoughtful mood as he studies the new Ford Can-Am engine during the 1969 series.

52

won the 1967 Le Mans and in 1963 A. J. captured both Nassau Speed Week features in the Mecom Scarab, Foyt's road racing career is limited. Three-time Indy winner Foyt leads all Speedway drivers with a lifetime total of 43 Championship Trail victories, but at 35, A. J. wants to win an unprecedented fourth '500' rather than race what he calls 'sporty cars.'

Mario Andretti's road racing reputation is based more on what he is believed capable of, than his record. In 1967 Mario won the Sebring 12 Hours co-driving the Ford Mk IV with Bruce McLaren and in 1968 he set a new lap record at Watkins Glen earning the pole for Lotus in the U.S. Grand Prix. But over and over again, driving Ferraris with Chris Amon at Monza and Sebring and in the Can-Am series, where his commitment to Ford keeps him saddled to questionable equipment, Mario has demonstrated his road racing savvy.

Twenty-nine-year-old Andretti did not leave the Trieste area until he was 13, Ascari and Fangio were his boyhood heroes and he has never outgrown his love of European racing. But, for the diminutive Italian immigrant to mount a proper Formula 1 challenge would greatly reduce his chance of retaining his National Championship. Mario's Indy winnings alone were $205,000.

The **Dan Gurney** saga is an American dream that did not quite come off. The handsome 38-year-old Californian has never realised his potential. Following almost instant success in West Coast sports car racing, Dan went to Europe in 1958 where he drove Ferraris at Le Mans and the Reims 12-Hour sports car race.

The next nine years saw Gurney with Ferrari, BRM, Porsche and Brabham Formula 1 factory rides. His 1962 victory in the French GP at Rouen was Dan's first and Porsche's only world championship success. Two years later he drove a Brabham, also in the French GP at Rouen, to Brabham's first-ever championship victory and before the lanky Californian turned away from Formula 1 he had notched six wins, including one in his own Anglo-

Andretti not so serious as he and Roger McCluskey clown in front of large 'blow-ups' of themselves.

American Eagle at Spa, the most world championships ever won by an American.

But Gurney's finishing record was spotty and he never acquired enough points to be a serious contender for the world driving title. Gurney's versatility is demonstrated by his having won five 500-mile stock car races as well as twice winning the Rex Mays 300 Indy car race. Dan finished second at Indy in 1968 and 1969 and brought his Indy Eagle home first in USAC races over road courses at Mosport and Donnybrooke.

Ranking 36-year-old Speedway veteran **Parnelli Jones** ahead of such U.S. road racing stalwarts as Mark Donohue and George Follmer is influenced by the 1963 Indy winner's performance in the Trans-Am series. While Parnelli won the 1964 Riverside GP driving Carroll Shelby's Cooper-Ford, it was not until Jones' Ford Mustang consistently earned the pole and frequently turned the fastest lap in the Trans-Am series that the road racing cognoscenti realised his worth.

Mark Donohue, a protégé of the late Walt Hans-gen, is American racing's Captain Nice. Quiet and considerate, the 32-year-old mechanical engineer came into his own when he joined former racing star, Roger Penske. After winning three Sports Car Club of America national titles Mark finished second in the 1966 Can-Am series and in 1967 and 1968 earned the U.S. Road Racing Championship. Donohue's Camaro won ten out of thirteen Trans-Ams in 1968 to bring Chevrolet the championship. Co-driving the Penske Lola-Chevy coupé with Chuck Parsons, Mark opened the 1969 season by winning the Daytona 24 Hours. Penske then decided to by-pass the Can-Am to concentrate on Indianapolis and the Trans-Am.

After a slow start Donohue won six Trans-Ams, five of them in a row, to give Camaro its second consecutive title. At the Speedway Mark qualified fourth and finished seventh to be named 1969 Indianapolis 'Rookie of the Year.'

By taking the 1969 Phoenix 150-miler, 36-year-old **George Follmer,** the 1965 U.S. Road Racing Champion, became one of the few sports car drivers

Canadian driver George Eaton, racing with BRM in 1970, spins off during the 1969 Can-Am series—and ducks down in his cockpit out of harm's way.

to win a USAC Championship race. After driving a factory Javelin in 1968, George drove a works Mustang in the 1969 Trans-Am where his furious inter-team battles with Parnelli Jones was one of the series highlights.

After several years of club racing in the States **Peter Revson,** 29-year-old bachelor member of the Revlon cosmetic family, barnstormed around Europe to learn his trade in the demanding school of Formula 3 and Formula 2 racing. Peter made his first trip to Indianapolis in 1969 where he qualified 33rd. He moved one of Jack Brabham's under-powered Repco-V-8's from last on the grid to finish fifth.

Revson drove a works Mustang in the 1969 Trans-Am series without success but in late July won the Indianapolis Raceway Park, USAC championship race in the Brabham-Repco. Peter joined his old rival Mark Donohue on the Javelin Trans-Am team in 1970.

Ronnie Bucknum, a 33-year-old Californian, joined the select cadre of road racers with victories on USAC oval tracks when he captured the 250-mile Indy car race at the Michigan Speedway inaugural in 1968. During 1969 Ronnie missed several months racing when he fell off his motor bike and later when his passenger car went off the road. But, as Donohue's partner in the Penske Camaros, the former Honda Formula 1 driver added his two Trans-Am victories to Donohue's six to give Chevrolet the championship.

At 43, oldest of U.S. road racing's big ten, **Chuck Parsons** is the single American to finish the 1969 Can-Am series with a creditable record. In 1969, Parsons, the 1966 U.S. Road Racing Champion, finished in the point-earning top ten in all but two

Motor racing is a grim business—or is it? (Top) William Cook captures the serious expression of Can-Am officials as they brief drivers before a race. But (below) International Motor Racing Book's 'man in America', Al Bochroch, seems to be happy enough at an 'after-the-race' party. Maybe it's just that reporters get all the fun and drivers do all the work? But Al's mellifluous tones are regularly heard covering motor sport over the Transatlantic airwaves.

of eleven Can-Ams to win a series total of $77,000. Chuck substituted for Ronnie Bucknum in the 1969 Daytona 24 Hours where he and Mark Donohue drove Penske's Lola coupé to a surprise win.

Twenty-five-year-old **Sam Posey** tops the list of U.S. comingmen. Scholarly, articulate Sam's 1969 season saw him drive Andy Granatelli's 4WD Plymouth to a fifth and a third in two Indy car road races. Substituting for Peter Revson, who was busy at Indy, Sam won the Lime Rock Trans-Am in a works Ford Mustang. Posey co-drove North American Racing Team Ferraris to class wins at the Daytona 24 Hours and Sebring as well as finishing eighth at Le Mans in the ancient Rindt-Gregory LM that won the 24 Hours in 1965. Formula A-5000 was Sam's major 1969 effort where his record shows two wins and three seconds. In 1970 Sam planned to concentrate on Indy and his new Trans-Am ride in a factory Dodge.

John Cannon, born in England 33 years ago, started his racing career in Canada. His outstanding drive was in the 1968 Monterey Can-Am which he won in a three-year-old McLaren. Cannon's victory over the rain-slicked Laguna Seca circuit was worth $19,550 and earned him a sponsored ride in the 1969 Formula A Continental series in which he has earned victories at Riverside, Sears Point and Mosport.

While remaining a Canadian citizen, Cannon now lives in Pasedena, California with his wife and two children.

The temptation to go beyond the top ten is strong. What about the brilliant young Canadian **George Eaton,** whose wealth and talent enabled him to finish fifth in the 1969 Can-Am series and get himself a 1970 Formula 1 ride with BRM. And the young German émigré **Lothar Motschenbacher,** who acts as Bruce McLaren's U.S. agent. Lothar was plagued with DNF's in the 1969 Can-Am but still managed to finish fifth of the eleven to capture seventh place in the series.

We omitted Chaparral designer-builder-driver **Jim Hall** as injuries, suffered late in 1968, forced the lanky Texan to sit-out the entire year. And we reluctantly pass-up hard-charging **Jerry Titus,** who made his Trans-Am Pontiac Firebird go

indecently fast, and steady **Tony Adamowicz,** leader of the Formula A forces.

While the United States Auto Club sanctions midget, sprint and stock cars as well as the Championship Trail series for Indy Cars, USAC is dominated by the '500'. Overseas driver representation in 1969 was limited to Denny Hulme and Jack Brabham when Chapman withdrew 1966 winner Graham Hill's and Jochen Rindt's Lotus 64's after suspension failures, although practice times indicated both would have qualified.

The starting grid consisted of Jack Brabham's and Revson's Repco-Brabham V-8's, Gurney's stock-block Ford, 19 turbocharged Offenhausers and 11 turbocharged Ford V-8's. While the field qualified at a record 166·295 m.p.h. average, Foyt's pole time was under Joe Leonard's Lotus-Turbine's 171·599 m.p.h. four-lap average set in 1968.

The 1969 '500' was almost all Andretti. Until the 440th mile Mario blazed a 160 m.p.h. race average. Gurney, Bobby Unser and Mel Kenyon finished almost two laps behind. Peter Revson, Joe Leonard, Mark Donohue and A. J. Foyt, who held an early lead until slowed by turbocharger trouble, completed the first eight of the sixteen finishers. Andretti's 156·867 m.p.h. race average was four m.p.h. over the old record. Mario's first '500' victory earned him 1,000 points towards winning his fourth USAC National Championship with a record total of 5,025 points, almost double that of Al Unser who finished second.

The Sports Car Club of America, sanctioning body for most U.S. road racing, began operating separate amateur and professional divisions in 1969. The amateur division sanctioned more than 300 club meets, drivers' schools, hill climbs and trials. Factory-supported Ford-Mustangs won the SCCA National Rally Championship, which, unfortunately, continues to reward split-second timing and the interpretation of tricky directions rather than driving and navigation skill.

Of the three pro series, the Canadian-American Challenge Cup and the Trans-American Sedan Championship pulled good crowds while the Formula A Continental single-seaters were more of an artistic than financial success. In 1969, its fourth

year, the Can-Am went from six to eleven races, three in Canada and eight in the U.S.

Bruce McLaren and Denny Hulme again dominated the series, winning all 11 races and pocketing $312,084 in total winnings. McLaren won six and was three times second while team-mate Hulme took the checker at five races and was second five times. Attendance exceeded 400,000 and prize money totalled $814,384. Chuck Parsons—Lola Chevy, Jo Siffert—Porsche 917, George Eaton—McLaren Chevy and Chris Amon—Ferrari 612, completed the first six places in final standings.

The best road racing in the United States during 1969 was the 12-race Trans-American Championship, a two-class series for manufacturers of up to 5 litre, and under 2 litre, sedans. Except in the U.S. the 305-cubic-inch, 5-litre, 2,900-pound, 116-inch wheelbase Trans-Am sedan would be considered a big car.

Ford, whose Mustang sired the 'pony-car' breed, won the title in 1966 and 1967 with factory-backed Mustangs. In 1968, the combination of Roger Penske's beautifully prepared Chevy-Camaros and Mark Donohue's driving brought the Trans-Am title to General Motors. To keep Penske from repeating Ford fielded two-car teams for Shelby Automotive and Bud Moore Eng. Carroll Shelby's regular drivers were Peter Revson and Horst Kwech, neither of whom won a race. However, Sam Posey drove Revson's Mustang to victory at Lime Rock while Peter was occupied at Indy.

Moore's drivers were 1963 Indy winner Parnelli Jones, who had two wins and four seconds, and 1965

U.S. Road Racing Champion George Follmer, who won once.

Following a slow start the Penske Camaros knocked-off seven straight wins to take the series, 78 points Chevrolet, 64 Ford. Penske, although a Chevrolet dealer, will run the AMC Javelin team in the 1970 Trans-Am and Peter Revson will join Mark Donohue.

With Dan Gurney and his protégé Swede Savage racing Plymouth Barracudas, Sam Posey in a works Dodge Challenger and Jim Hall taking on the chore of defending the title for Camaro, the 1970 Trans-Am should be better than ever. Trans-Am racing is colourful, noisy, rich and violent. In many ways, some of them unfortunate, it is typical of America.

The late model stock cars that slam over the steeply banked ovals of the American South-east enjoyed another record breaking year. David Pearson's Ford Torino captured the Grand National Championship but LeeRoy Yarbrough, was stock cars big money winner. By concentrating on 400- and 500-mile events over the super speedways at Daytona, Darlington and Rockingham, LeeRoy earned a record $188,605 for seven victories, against Pearson's $183,700.

Second in Grand National points is Richard Petty, who leaves Ford and returns to Plymouth for the 1970 season, while Cale Yarborough, 1968's top winner, is expected to miss much of the 1970 season nursing a shoulder injury.

Ford, with 375 points and 26 victories, nosed-out Dodge for the NASCAR Manufacturers' Championship.

Mark Donohue in his Trans-Am winning Camaro during the 1969 series. He is driving Javelin this year.

The mighty power of the big American cars seen in this shot by Al Bochroch (top). In the leading car is LeeRoy Yarbrough, NASCAR top dollar earner in 1969 with a take of $200,000. Yarbrough won seven major stock-car victories, his nearest rival being David Pearson, who won the Grand National Championship but finished several thousand dollars behind Yarbrough in the money stakes. (Below) another outstanding driver on the U.S. and Canadian circuits, George Drolson.

J O is Swiss. He owns a garage business near Fribourg which is located in the French part of this little European country. Jo earns a lot of money—partly through his business (the garage buys and sells fancy big-capacity automobiles), partly through motor racing as he is one of the most demanded racing drivers of today. Still, Jo remains a friendly, modest person—despite tremendous success in his motor-racing career.

It started in 1957 when Siffert had been an apprentice in a garage business: he bought himself a 125-c.c. Gilera motor-cycle and did some racing for mere fun. Later he changed to bigger motor-cycles and then became the Swiss National Champion in the 350-c.c. class in 1959—two years after he had started racing!

At that time Jo didn't earn much money. His racing activity could only be financed by a frugal way of living. He slept in tents when out racing, ate little and saved every penny he could. Thus he started his own little business—buying and selling cars and motor-cycles—allowing him to acquire a second-hand Stanguellini Formula Junior racing car in 1960.

The young racing driver didn't bother to compete in national races. He'd rather finish a race in a rear position than go to second-class meetings with more chances for good placings. Soon his uncompetitive

car was sold after some minor successes (sixth at Reims, fourth at Messina). In 1961 Jo was regarded as the best driver on the Continent in the Formula Junior. Now in a Lotus 20, he won no less than eight international races that year. After another successful season Jo decided to go Formula 1.

Nobody offered him a chance in a works team. The only way to participate in the top branch of motor sport was to go to England and buy a car. His business was already doing well by then and nothing could stop the Swiss from acting. His newly acquired Lotus-BRM was taken to Monaco and Siffert managed to qualify for the Grand Prix—indeed, he was faster than Jim Hall and even Maurice Trintignant. Mechanical failure forced Jo out of this race. His next race, the Belgian Grand Prix, was without luck again. Jo spun off the road. However, in his first year of Grand Prix racing Joseph still scored two points towards the World Championship.

1964: Jo now drove a Brabham-BRM. He was fourth in the German Grand Prix and third in the US Grand Prix. Rob Walker decided to give this talented driver a chance in his team.

1965: Siffert's placings were convincing—sixth at Monaco, sixth at the French Grand Prix, fourth in Mexico.

1966: In the first year of the new 3-litre Formula 1

Siffert was slightly less successful than expected due to many mechanical failures with his heavy Cooper-Maserati. In another type of racing, however, Jo was given a chance which later gave this team the championship title: Sports car racing in Porsches. In a Carrera 6 Siffert won his class at Le Mans already this year, in fact he finished fourth overall.

1967: In the Walker Grand Prix car Siffert finished twice in fourth position. His Cooper-Maserati was no longer competitive against the new lightweight machinery from Lotus, Brabham or Ferrari. Therefore, his luck was better in the Sports car category. He was fourth at Sebring, fifth at Monza, second at Spa, fifth at the Targa Florio,

fifth at Le Mans (winning Porsche the Index of Performance) and third at Brands Hatch. Gradually, it became obvious how good a racing driver he was, once in a more competitive car. Also Siffert usually finished a race—his treatment of the delicate machinery was excellent.

In the meantime, Jo became somewhat a national hero in his home country, in Switzerland. Circuit racing has been banned from this country for years. The countless race fans had to go abroad and watch foreigners win big-time races. Swiss names hardly appeared even on the starting lists. And here was a young Swiss, a likeable character everybody could approach and talk to, someone who went up the

61

A dramatic head-on shot of Jo Siffert's Porsche during the 1969 BOAC 500 at Brands Hatch, Kent.

Top: Jo Siffert gets the chequered flag as he wins the 1969 Austrian Thousand Kilometres race. Below: Siffert (No. 4) and Pedro Rodriguez (No. 2) lapping Hanrioud (No. 34) in the 1969 Monza Thousand Kilometres race. Siffert has established an outstanding reputation as a long-distance specialist.

steep ladder of motor racing, all by himself. Jo Siffert was now a name even the uninitiated would know.

1968: Rob Walker decided to swap his now old-fashioned Cooper for more competitive machinery. Rob bought a Lotus 49. The first race with the new car looked promising: Jo was in the second row on the starting grid and held second position during the race until the transmission failed and Jo had to call it a day.

In the Belgian Grand Prix Jo was seventh. Jo complained about the car's handling. Rob Walker complained that the new car—the Lotus 49B—had not yet been delivered to him while the works cars were such new types.

Finally, in England, Siffert's efforts in Formula 1 were crowned. He shared the front position on the grid with the established World Champion Graham Hill, young Jack Oliver and Chris Amon. When the flag dropped, Oliver shot into the lead, Hill was second and then came Jo. Hill dropped out first. This left Oliver in front. Behind him Amon and Siffert were dicing for second place. Siffert succeeded. Then Oliver retired. Jo was leading with Amon behind him pressing on. Now all eyes were on the Swiss driver who went just fast enough not to get caught by Amon but not fast enough to risk mechanical trouble. Jo remained in front. He won his first Grand Prix—in a privately-owned car!

Later that year, at Monza, Jo was trying to catch the leader, Denny Hulme, when his rear suspension collapsed and ended a hopeful race that could have been another Grand Prix victory.

Whenever Jo had the right machinery, he proved that he belongs to the top-class in Grand Prix racing.

But there is no doubt whatsoever that he belongs to the crème de la crème of Sports car racing. There he has had the proper works cars, there he has proved beyond doubt who he is. His record in 1968: second (funnily enough: first as well since the Porsche team manager put Jo into the winning car after his car had dropped out when leading) at Daytona, first at Sebring, first at the Nürburgring. In most other Sports car championship races Siffert dropped out due to mechanical trouble when being in front positions.

Out in front at the beautiful wooded circuit of the Nürburg-ring. Siffert stayed there to win the 1000 Kilometres race.

His best year was 1969! Now Siffert was familiar with the Porsches—Porsche was familiar with the driver, too. Together with the superb British driver, Brian Redman—an ideal pair in ideal machinery—he won Porsche the championship title for makes. Siffert's records in 1969 included: first at Brands Hatch, first at Monza, first at Spa, first at the Nürburgring, first at Watkins Glen. Out of ten championship races Siffert had won five. When Siffert did not show up in the first position at the end of a race he had usually dropped out for technical reasons. Practice times prove Jo's ability: third at Daytona, fourth at Sebring, first at Brands, second at Monza, third at Spa, first at the Nürburgring, third at Le Mans, first at Watkins Glen and fourth at Zeltweg. On the Grand Prix point table Jo ranked ninth this year, in front of the likes of Brabham, Surtees and Amon. Fortune was against Jo again. Out of 11 Grand Prix races Siffert had to sideline his car six times—mechanical failures the reason.

In the Canadian-American Challenge Cup Siffert appeared mid-season with a 4·5-litre Porsche, based on the Sports car type 917. The car was still too heavy, compared with the rival machinery, and it was extremely underpowered. Most competitors don't dare to put engines with less than 6,000 c.c. into their Can-Am chassis, some of them competed with 7- or even 8-litre power plants. Siffert beat most of them: he finished fourth on the final point

table, behind the two McLarens (McLaren and Hulme) and behind Chuck Parsons who had driven a 7-litre Lola-Chevrolet.

When time allowed, Siffert also drove a Formula 2 BMW, together with his team-mate there, Hubert Hahne. It goes without saying that, once the car was in perfect condition—which, unfortunately, was seldom—Jo was out in front with the top people like Stewart, Rindt, Courage and so on.

In 1969 Joseph Siffert participated in over 30 major races—not including less important single events, and apart from the uncounted days of practice, testing and other commitments in this sport. Despite lack of time it seldom happens that Jo won't answer questions to either his friends or journalists. Jo is known for his good humour. If, for example, a journalist asks him silly questions, Jo is usually well prepared to give him a very silly answer as well.

Although he is a determined driver—some of his colleagues even fear his 'wild driving'—Jo likes to enjoy life. He's not 'afraid' of parties.

The Swiss driver is very much liked among his colleagues; there was hardly one Grand Prix driver who didn't say how pleased he had been to see Jo Siffert win the British Grand Prix in 1968. But in the past two to three years Siffert's style of driving has changed somewhat. Jo was always known as a talented and extremely brave driver, yet his performance was usually much unnoticed by the public —he appeared to be driving rather calmly and not spectacularly.

Nowadays one can find his car going sideways quite frequently, clipping kerbs, throwing sand and gravel.

When the starting flag drops Jo is determined to snatch the best place possible right from the beginning. His tyres throw up a lot of smoke from the spinning rear wheels. He looks devilishly frightening during the early stages of a race and if he is dicing for positions even at the end of it.

But once the race is over he's the same quiet, friendly person as ever.

Asked once, whether he feels unsafe going through the corners sideways, Jo said: 'Oh no—I'm perfectly safe—it is all a matter of practising this.'

Siffert and co-driver Brian Redman discuss the situation as their car is refuelled during the 1969 BOAC 500.

the name of the game
is WINNING

The Players

The Story

FRANK CAPUA, one of the top racing drivers in America, has just won the Redburne 200, one of the most important sports car races in the United States. Second to finish is Luther Erding while third is Les Bottineau. The three, fierce competitors on the track, are friends otherwise and carry on their racing wars all over the country.

As is the case after all races, there is a huge celebration in Redburne and Frank soon wearies of being chased and caught by people of all ages. Women, both young and old, want to kiss or mother him. The men and boys want his autograph or tickets to the next race. So Capua slips away from the party and into the night.

He goes into a car rental office where he meets Elora, the most attractive woman in town. He suggests she should drive him around. The two leave together. She is divorced, lives with her 13-year-old son Charley, and mother. She is lonely, so is Capua. They like each other, go to California, where Frank lives, and soon get married.

Frank's next race is at Riverside, a stock car race in which he fails to finish when his car spins and flips. Frank is unhurt. Then comes Minneapolis, and Frank again loses as Erding manages to block him off and win himself. Erding is triumphant at the victory.

Frank's bad luck follows him to the San Francisco stock car races, where he is forced out of the race. And then comes Trenton, another stock car event. This time Frank's car breaks down and once again he is forced out and leaves the victory for Erding to pick up.

66

Clu Gulager advises Robert Wagner (above) and (op runs on to the track to help his drivers after a crash.

As the important Indy 500 draws near, Leo Crawford, a race car builder, signs Capua and Erding to drive two of his specially built cars in the race. By this time, both Frank and Erding are in the real money. Also, by this time Frank has adopted Elora's son, who looks up to Frank as a hero as well as a friend.

Frank, Elora and Erding move into Indianapolis a month before the race to prepare the cars for time trials, both shooting for the pole position for the qualifying runs. While they work on the cars and test them, Erding and Elora are surprised by Frank who finds them in the midst of an affair at their motel. All three keep a tight clamp on their emotions and there is no outward blow-up.

Erding's car is made ready for the first time trial. He is determined to win the pole position and pushes the car far beyond normal. The car suddenly seems to explode in the first lap of the trial and has to be hosed down and wheeled off the track. At this point, Crawford tells Capua he is going to have Erding drive the second car that same day in another attempt to qualify. His reasoning is simply that Frank has been running in hard luck lately, Erding on a winning streak.

Told he will not be allowed to drive the car originally intended for him, Frank tells Crawford to find another car and walks off. Erding qualifies in the

second car later that day, gaining spot number four.

That night young Charley arrives in town, having hitch-hiked from Redburne. He has come to see Frank because he loves him and because his mother has told him they were not getting along in their marriage. The boy tells Frank he came to see him beat Erding in the 500.

Frank thinks it over, then decides to rebuild the first car Erding drove. He tells Crawford, who is delighted. With the help of Larry Morchek, Crawford's chief mechanic, the rebuilding gets under way and the following Saturday Frank qualifies the car in 16th position.

The big race day begins with a spectacular 17-car accident on the very first lap. Luckily, there are no fatalities, just a batch of cars out of the race. Erding is forced to pit early in the race when his engine starts to miss. The crew replaces a faulty plug and he's back on the track again. Frank's car, meanwhile, is working beautifully and he's driving with all his vast skill and knowledge. He moves up, up and up, ever closer to the lead. When he finally pits, he is in fifth position, driving strong.

Erding, too, is giving it all he has but it proves not enough. His motor suddenly cuts out with less than 25 laps to go and he is abruptly out of the race. Stepping out of the car in the infield, his rage and fury are awesome, and he literally kicks the car out of shape. Frank just pours it on, picking up car after car until there is but one in front. His old pal, Les Bottineau. The two are locked in a tense, wheel-to-wheel duel. Frank drives on to victory.

The following day, as Frank is about to check out of his motel, Erding appears to say he is sorry about the trouble he caused and that there is no feeling between him and Elora. Frank listens, then explodes and fights with Erding.

Frank's world is now desolate. His big victory empty and meaningless. The thought cuts through the pained, lonely haze torturing Frank and he heads towards the house—and Elora. She is waiting for him. Together they decide it's worth a fresh start.

A Universal/Newman-Foreman Picture, distributed by the Rank Organisation. Directed by James Goldstone and produced by John Foreman. In Technicolour and Panavision.

Paul Newman in his role as Frank Capua in the film production 'Winning' in which he co-stars with his wife, Joanne Woodward.

RACES I REMEMBER

By DENNY HULME

MOTOR racing is a non-stop business these days, with events taking place all over the world all round the year. There is now no real closed season for the sport, and inevitably I have my fair share of races every year. Some of these I thoroughly enjoy, some I find rather boring, and some I positively hate. Sometimes everything goes right from start to finish, sometimes nothing goes as it should, and occasionally there is either disappointment or delight just when it is least expected.

But out of all my races, just a few stand out in my memory as something special. They're not necessarily races I've won (though they're usually the ones that are easiest to remember) but they have a quality that sets them apart. Indeed, one of my most vivid

incidents happened in practice. This was at Clermont Ferrand, training for the French Grand Prix in 1965. It was only my second Grand Prix (the first had been at Monaco a month earlier when I finished eighth) but I'd been to the Charade circuit previously for Formula 2 races and I knew it pretty well.

On the first day of practice I managed to set the quickest time against some really hot opposition. You can't imagine what this meant to me at that stage. I knew that I had gone well because I knew the circuit so well, but all the same it showed me that I didn't have to be daunted by drivers like Jim Clark, Jackie Stewart, Dan Gurney and Graham Hill.

In the end, of course, the greater experience of my

rivals relegated me to the third row of the starting-grid—I was sixth fastest—but I was pretty happy about it in my second GP, and it gave me confidence for the race.

I remember that I didn't make a very good start, and I had quite a battle with John Surtees, who was in a Ferrari. In view of my inexperience in Formula 1 it was obvious that the best policy was to play things quietly and not do anything ridiculous. In the end this brought me fourth place, and three world championship points.

By the end of the season my total was a mere five championship points, but those first three points and that first-day practice time were the greatest things in the world for me.

Another outstanding memory is a race I didn't win. In fact, I could only finish fourth, but it was the first time I led a Grand Prix from the start, and by three-quarters distance it seemed to be in the bag . . . when disaster struck.

This was the South African GP at Kyalami in January, 1967 when I was partnering Jack Brabham in his Brabham-Repco team. Our cars had gone extremely well in practice; Jack was in pole position and I was alongside him on the front row at the start. When the flag fell everything clicked, and I shot away in front of the pack.

On lap three, when Jack spun off, I had a lead of around five seconds and from then I found it possible to pull away from the rest of the field. After 40 laps—half distance—I had a minute's lead on the second man, and I remember telling myself that all I had to do was to slow down and take it steady.

The car clearly had plenty in hand; I'd set a new record lap on lap three when the fuel tanks were nearly full, and the engine was running as smooth as a nut. Then around the sixtieth lap I suddenly realised I was having to pump the brake pedal, first once and then on the next lap round a couple of times. This was followed by a sudden disappearance of my brakes altogether.

I thought to myself, 'No, this just can't be true.' I rushed into the pits, shouting to the mechanics to get some brake fluid ready, and came in again next time round. They topped up the master cylinders, but soon found this hadn't cured things. So I was in again three laps later, when it was discovered the brakes couldn't be bled, and so I soldiered on without any anchors.

It was a terrifying ride, using the gearbox all I could to slow down for the corners, though this is not easy after rushing down the straight at over 160 m.p.h., and without brakes you daren't corner so quickly for fear that if something goes wrong you have no control.

So one minute I thought I had nine championship points, and very soon I had only got three. It was disappointing all right, but it was a race to remember. Since it was, in fact, the opening race which was to lead to my world championship, it was also a milestone.

like a hero. There is no doubt that the Monaco Grand Prix is regarded as one of the greatest races in the calendar, so it was especially sweet to make it my first GP win on that fabulous circuit.

Things went well during practice, except that it wasn't until late in the final training session that I got my car to handle to my liking and so get a useful place on the grid. The Monaco circuit is tight and narrow, and it's just as well to be near the front at the start. Anyway, I was on the second row of the two-by-two grid, alongside John Surtees in his Honda, and we were behind Jack (who was quickest of all)

But even more of a milestone came in the next Grand Prix, at Monaco, when I achieved my great ambition of winning a world championship race. After the disappointment in South Africa, I couldn't help feeling there was some justice after all!

That victory at Monaco was probably the biggest booster to my morale I have ever had. I well remember that the following day I was over in Indianapolis, getting ready for the famous 500-mile race there, and everyone seemed to be treating me

and Lorenzo Bandini, the brilliant Ferrari driver.

Jack ran into trouble immediately, and dropped a lot of oil when his engine blew up, but in fact this gave me something of an advantage because my car felt good on oil. Jackie Stewart got past me at the Gasometer hairpin, slipping through on the inside, and then began to pull away. He was driving well, but then his BRM broke its crownwheel and pinion, and so I inherited a useful lead. Then Jim Clark—whom I was most anxious about—and some of my

72

Former world champion Hulme in typical action during the 1969 RAC British Grand Prix at Silverstone, Northants.

other rivals started to close the gap, and at the time there seemed nothing I could do about it.

Jim, who never won the Monaco GP in all his glorious career, was out of luck again, and had to retire after a rear damper mounting broke and he hit the wall coming out of Tabac corner.

Bandini was really flying, and was catching me at the rate of half a second a lap. Somehow, I just wasn't switched on; I was going round reasonably fast but not as fast as I should have been. Then I got a pits signal telling me that Bandini was only seven seconds behind, and all of a sudden I got with it again, trying to make sure he didn't get any nearer, because I knew that once he saw me ahead on the road he would have an added incentive.

This race, of course, was overshadowed with tragedy, for Bandini crashed at the chicane, his Ferrari caught fire, and he died from his injuries a few days later. Maybe he had been trying a bit too hard in an effort to catch me, maybe he was getting tired—Monaco is a very tiring circuit and he had missed a gear occasionally just before he went off at the chicane. At the time, of course, we didn't know how seriously injured he was. It was a momentous race for me, but a tragic one as well.

That same month came another race which stands out in my memory—my first effort in the Indianapolis 500. I was very raw and inexperienced in this very different sort of racing. As a newcomer I had to take a carefully checked rookie test, gradually increasing speeds according to instructions. Naturally, the race itself was a big occasion for me, and it wasn't made any easier for me when rain came down and we had to start all over again the next day. I settled down in around fifteenth position, determined to play it cool while I learned all I could.

By half distance I had moved up to seventh place, but dropped back to tenth after a fuel stop.

Then I suddenly found myself seventh again. In fact, it's not at all easy to discover what is happening; you are completely dependent on pit signals because you don't really know who you are passing or who is overtaking you. You just keep going and cross your fingers that you're doing well.

I saw Jackie Stewart walking back to the pits and learned I was fifth. Then I saw the fantastic turbine-

Aerofoils still in fashion in the 1969 Spanish Grand Prix with Hulme, Surtees and McLaren well to the fore.

73

powered car driven by Parnelli Jones in trouble (he had been romping home in the lead but retired with only four laps to go) and knew I had moved up another place. On the second to last lap we had been on the amber light (which means no-one is allowed to change his position) and I was hoping it would stay like that until the finish to make certain of my fourth place. But the light suddenly flashed to green again, and I accelerated behind Al Unser—who was second—as he pulled out to overtake a bunch of cars. The next thing I knew was the amber light was on again and four cars behind me had all disappeared.

It was obvious there had been an accident, so the next time round I trod carefully, and sure enough the track seemed to be completely blocked with wreckage. I knocked the car out of gear and let it tick over as I picked my way through the debris, and then, to my relief, saw my entrant waving me to cross the finish line.

It was a relief, and I was very pleased to be fourth. They made me Rookie of the Year for that performance, which made me even more pleased because it is a highly regarded honour. Certainly a race to remember.

That was quite a momentous season for me, and the German Grand Prix in August was another race I still treasure when I look back. I remember it not only because it brought me my second Grand Prix victory but also because the car went so well round the tough Nürburgring circuit. On my two previous visits there I had managed a total of only nine laps, so this was a welcome change, and it was particularly pleasing because the German Grand Prix was high on the list of races I wanted to win. The Nürburgring circuit is probably more scaring than difficult, with all its corners and many of them with a blind approach. There just isn't any room for mistakes at the 'Ring.

On the first lap of the race three of us—Jim Clark, Dan Gurney and myself—quickly lost all the others. Jim had his Lotus in the lead and I tucked in behind to get a tow in his slipstream. That tow lasted for three laps, and continued for a while later when Dan slipped by with his Eagle. On lap four Jim was in trouble; I knew he was having problems because he kept looking over his shoulder to see what was wrong with his car. In fact, his suspension was going, and he had to give up.

After Dan and I slipped past the Lotus we had a

tight struggle, but though I did all I knew it simply wasn't possible to lose the Eagle. Dan got by me when I got all crossed up in landing from the big all-wheels-off jump on the far side of the circuit, and then he started to pull away. His car was going very well, and I had to resign myself to seeing him disappear into the distance. He got 45 seconds ahead of me, and set a new record lap in the process, but unfortunately the Eagle had a drive shaft break and so I inherited a 45-second lead with three laps to go. This was a comforting situation, but three laps of the 14-miles-plus 'Ring was still a long way to go.

I concentrated on keeping going quickly while saving the car as much as possible, changing up early every time to keep the revs down. Fortunately, the engine never missed a beat all the way to the chequered flag, and I was very grateful for the wonderful way the mechanics had prepared the car.

The car suffered no damage during the race, but when I stepped out of the cockpit I broke the windscreen. But nobody minded that, because Jack Brabham brought the other team car into second place to make it a splendid day for us.

When I come to think about it, 1967 was quite a year, for I had my first race in the Can-Am series . . . and won. I was driving one of Bruce McLaren's new M6A cars, and this was the start of an association that later brought some convincing results in this very rich Can-Am series of races in Canada and the United States.

Bruce had put a lot of effort into these cars, but we went to the first race, at Elkhart Lake, feeling rather apprehensive; we were confident that our M6As were quick but we didn't know what the opposition would produce. But practice was very encouraging, and in the race I managed to lead from start to finish.

It was a trouble-free outing, and not too tough, but I remember it because it marked the start of three years during which Bruce and I managed to dominate the series.

Going back much earlier, though, there are one or two other races that still give me a glow when I recall them. One was the Vic Hudson Memorial Trophy at Levin in my native New Zealand in 1960. I drove a 2-litre Cooper-Climax, and won the race.

It was a good dice and my first big win. It was important, too, because it attracted the attention of the New Zealand International Grand Prix Association, and they sent me to Britain to learn more about racing. They paid my fare and living expenses and I landed in England in April of that year. I didn't realise then just what it would lead to. I had ambitions like so many other drivers, but deep down I don't think I ever thought it would be possible to get the breaks and become world champion.

Another step along the road came at Brands Hatch on Boxing Day at the end of 1962. I'd been working at Jack Brabham Motors, carrying out conversions on Alpines and Rapiers, and keeping my ears cocked in case there was a chance of a drive in Jack's early Formula Junior car. I did get a chance during the summer when the regular driver was out of action following an accident; this was at Crystal Palace, where I remember setting fastest practice time and finishing fourth in the race. But on Boxing Day there came the opportunity of another go in the car, and this time I won. The outcome was that Jack signed me to drive for him for the 1963 season.

It was more than two years before I landed my first Grand Prix drive, but that Boxing Day race was a turning point that eventually led to bigger things. So I'll always remember it with affection.

SOME motor racing circuits seem to gain a special place in the hearts of followers of the sport. Inevitably, in pre-war days Brooklands was such a place and in the post-war world it was Goodwood which seemed to succeed to the Brooklands mantle. Now, like its Weybridge predecessor, the lovely Sussex circuit has ceased operations and, before the memory fades, Graham Macbeth recalls some of the great races, the great drivers and the great days which made it 'glorious Goodwood'. Macbeth, a longtime official of the British Automobile Racing Club and presently Press Officer at Brands Hatch, is also the motoring correspondent of the Brighton Evening Argus. Few have better qualifications to recall . . . .

THE GLORY
THAT WAS
GOODWOOD

TODAY when Bruce McLaren laps the 2.4 miles of Goodwood motor-racing circuit at over 125 m.p.h. in his Can-Am sports car, few people outside the McLaren team really care. A little over 20 years ago, when the circuit first came to life, nobody would have believed it possible.

Indeed, the whole project seemed a bit beyond the bounds of possibility when it first started to happen. The post-war motor-racing scene was not so much dim as virtually non-existent. Brooklands, that pre-war Mecca of British motor racing, had disappeared—sold out to an aircraft company to the bitter disgust of the motor-racing types, who genuinely thought that they had been cheated.

Goodwood had been a piece of farmland in pre-war days but in the early 1940s had become a satellite to nearby Tangmere aerodrome and the home of fighter aircraft. It was a pilot, Squadron-Leader Tony Gaze, who first suggested to the Duke of Richmond and Gordon, another RAF type, that motor racing should take place at Westhampnett, as the airfield was known, after the adjacent village.

His Grace, one of the better known and more successful Brooklands drivers in his younger days as the Earl of March, was at first stunned by the thought of a race circuit on part of the estate of his ancestral home, a mile or two from the other famous Goodwood course where his family had run horse-racing for some 150 years.

But there was tremendous enthusiasm and on 18 September, 1948, that Goodwood motor course came to life—just two weeks before the RAC ran its first post-war Grand Prix at Silverstone.

That funny little Goodwood meeting, with seven three-lap races and a 'big' race of five laps, was the start of a new tradition and could be said to mark the birth of British motor racing in its present world-beating form.

In retrospect, it was incredibly casual. The starter's rostrum was a step-ladder and the spectator 'protection' was a width of grass and a length of rope.

Yet, immediately, Goodwood was to start establishing trends which were to transform the very shape of motor racing throughout the world. The first person to lap the Goodwood course in under two minutes was a young lad called Stirling Moss,

just 18 years old, and the car he drove was a Cooper, a make which was to revolutionise racing car design.

Goodwood had a lot to commend it. Although an airfield track, with all the limitations which that normally entails in flatness and lack of natural features, it was superbly situated below the Sussex Downs and the people who ran it were, for much of its career at least, highly enthusiastic and able to back their enthusiasm with money. When they made more money, they ploughed it back into the circuit to carry out improvements.

The Brooklands tradition was strong at Goodwood. They even set up a Brooklands Memorial Garden, which included a piece of concrete banking from the old Weybridge track and, with just two exceptions (an all-Vintage car race and the one-and-only motor cycle meeting) every race meeting at Goodwood was organised by the British Automobile Racing Club, which, as the Junior Car Club, was one of the main Brooklands clubs of pre-war days.

Although they perpetuated strange rites like Brooklands-style handicap races, the BARC generally advanced with the new form of British motor racing which it did much to establish. In only a few years it was easily the most influential club in the country, with the world's largest membership for a motor-racing club and, in the late '50s, a far more extensive programme of major events than any other club, not to mention a worthy selection of club races which soon began to produce new drivers of the highest calibre.

One such was Mike Hawthorn, the blond giant who became the first British world champion driver. In a pre-war Riley sports car tuned by his father, Hawthorn was the club champion of 1951, winning the *Motor Sport* Brooklands Memorial Challenge Trophy in a points championship at Goodwood Members' meetings—the first significant clubman's championship in the history of modern British motor racing.

By 1952, Goodwood's Easter Monday International Meeting had become the traditional season opener of British racing and it was the young Hawthorn who made the headlines, winning two races (beating the reigning world champion Fangio in the

77

process) with the new 2-litre Cooper-Bristol Formula 2 car and being runner-up to Gonzales in the 4½-litre Thin Wall Special Ferrari in the day's main event. That was some début in international racing!

But it was Stirling Moss who was the most consistently great driver on the Sussex track. From his first success at the opening meeting, he soon became the top 500 c.c. driver and rapidly moved on to more powerful machinery.

Moss had wins in a variety of cars, such as the works Maserati in which he enjoyed a tremendous battle with Hawthorn's BRM and Scott-Brown's Connaught in 1956 and the Cooper with which, in 1959, he beat that year's champion, Jack Brabham, but it was in Goodwood's only World Championship races, the sports car RAC Tourist Trophy events, that, at Goodwood, Moss lived up to the reputation he earned elsewhere.

Moss won the TT seven times in all—three times in Northern Ireland and four times in a row at Goodwood.

The second of the Goodwood TT wins was a real triumph in the face of adversity. Whilst leading, the Aston Martin being shared by Moss and Salvadori burst into flames when an over-eager mechanic sprayed the car with petrol before getting the filler nozzle into the tank during a routine pit stop. The open pipe was dropped into the middle of the fire and another 50 gallons of fuel was added to the horrifying blaze.

The pits themselves caught fire but the race went on while Goodwood's own estate fire brigade tackled the flames. Moss took over the Carroll Shelby/Jack Fairman Aston Martin and regained the lead to ensure that the team also won the World Sports Car Championship of 1959.

It was the second big pits fire at Goodwood, the first having been in the 1952 Nine-Hours sports car race (Britain's first event with racing after dark) and again it was an Aston Martin—the Reg Parnell/Eric Thompson car—which went up in smoke, but the Peter Collins/Pat Griffith sister model won the race.

Indeed, open Aston Martin cars won each of the three highly exciting but financially unsuccessful *News of the World* sponsored Nine-Hours races in 1952, 1953 and 1955 and the first two Goodwood TTs in 1958-9. It was not until the TT became a Grand Touring car race that Aston Martins' series of long distance successes at Goodwood came to an end and the last five Goodwood TT races went to Ferrari.

The first two of these, in 1960 and 1961, were both

won by Moss in a Ferrari 250GT entered by Rob Walker. The 1961 race was Stirling's last Goodwood win. On Easter Monday, 1962, he had a terrible accident which finished his racing career and, like his international début, it was at Goodwood. In a Formula 1 race in which he had made two pit stops with his Lotus, Moss was two laps behind the BRM of leader (and eventual winner) Graham Hill, embarking on his first championship year.

Perhaps aiming at a new lap record (he had already established a joint record with John Surtees earlier in the race), Moss appeared to attempt to overtake Hill. The Lotus left the track, careered across the grass and smote the earth bank on the outside of the circuit.

It took nearly half-an-hour to get Moss out of the dreadfully smashed and petrol-soaked car. He was removed, near to death, with severe head injuries which, he decided later, had slowed down his reactions so much that he has not raced seriously since. At the time, Goodwood was probably the only circuit in the country equipped with a full rescue kit which later became obligatory at all circuits. But for this precaution by the safety-conscious Goodwood

79 *Moss's last race at Goodwood. He chases Graham Hill (BRM) through the chicane then crashes at St Mary's Corner.*

authorities and the BARC, Moss could well have died before being released from his car.

At Goodwood, they had soon rid themselves of their nightmares of potential crowd slaughter which could have resulted from the original grass verge and rope spectator protection of 1948. While other tracks pinned their faith on straw bales, or a sloping grassy bank fronted by a shallow ditch, Goodwood soon blossomed forth with an entire encirclement of vertical reinforced concrete barriers which were a bit rough on the cars but about as safe as possible for

Goodwood was also the first British track to have entirely covered paddock stalls (few others have them to this day). It also had four 40-foot high observation towers at strategic points to supplement the normal marshals' posts (each of which had a raised cabin with toilet room beneath, and all protected by fortress-like concrete emplacements).

White-painted fences made the paddock smart, flower beds adorned the track-side in the start area and, with some of the grandeur of the nearby horse-racing course rubbing off onto the motor track,

The start of it all. Lew Ebblewhite (opposite) uses a stepladder as a starter's rostrum to flag off Goodwood's first ever race, won by Pycroft (Jaguar). Spectator protection (above) consisted of a width of grass and a length of rope. The infield was cultivated to the very edge of the track.

drivers (who seldom suffered injury, as cars hit the barriers with a glancing blow). Moss was very unlucky in going off at one of the few parts of the Goodwood track where it was possible to hit the bank head on. It was a prohibited area to spectators with no deflecting vertical barriers.

When, in preparation for the 1952 Nine-Hours race, pits were erected for the first time, they thought far enough ahead to introduce the notorious chicane, a very artificial S bend, to make sure that cars were slowed to a safe speed before the pit area. The Goodwood chicane infuriated the purists but spectators loved it and half the stands were in its vicinity.

there was a special VIP lunch room and viewing stand built into the Race Control block.

Vehicle and pedestrian tunnels were built under the track to provide access during practice and racing, avoiding the infuriating delays which can cause so much bad feeling when this access is not available.

In its heyday, they did things in style at Goodwood. There was a social atmosphere unlike anything in motor racing before or since. The Duke's stately home in the park near the track, with the lovely old Richmond Arms pub at its gate, was the scene of cocktail parties on the evenings before each

The main race at the first meeting had a field of nine cars running over five laps. The fastest lap was put up by Bob Gerard (ERA) (No. 21) but the race was won by Reg Parnell (Maserati 4CLT). Above: the scene at the start. Below: the winner crosses the finishing-line.

of the big race meetings. On the fine pitch in front of Goodwood House there were charity cricket matches in which Grand Prix drivers challenged the local team (both aided by the odd County cricketer or two) in hilarious games enlivened by a race commentator's remarks over a public address system.

When the airfield was reopened so that the growing number of pilots among the motor racing fraternity could fly into their favourite track, the Royal Aero Club marked the occasion with a rally. No fewer than 75 aircraft invaded Goodwood, which coped with the unexpected problems a bit better than the airport authorities at Croydon, where most of the 'planes appeared as a single flock at sunset, all wanting to land during the last few minutes of failing light, whereas at Goodwood they had gone down over a period of several hours!

Virtually everyone who was anyone in racing competed at Goodwood. In the early days, the star was Reg Parnell with a 4CLT Maserati. Similar cars were raced by Prince Bira of Siam, Baron E. (Barney) de Graffenreid, of Switzerland, and the first officially-recognised world champion, Dr Giuseppe Farina, of Italy.

The first outright lap record, however, went to Bob Gerard's ERA in 1 minute 43.6 seconds—83.4 m.p.h. In 1949, Parnell got the record as well as the race wins and left the new mark at 87.10 m.p.h. By the end of the season it was Parnell's again at 89.26 m.p.h. With wet days for the big races of 1950, Parnell's record stood intact but 1951 saw tremendous speed increases. Bira cracked 90 in the 4½-litre Osca on Easter Monday and Parnell followed this at Whitsun with 94.53 m.p.h. in the Thin Wall Ferrari but at the end of the season, Farina was back, this time in the 1½-litre Alfa Romeo 158 on one of its final outings. It was still the quickest thing yet seen at Goodwood and the immaculate Farina took it round at a then astonishing 97.36 m.p.h.

During the winter, the course was altered by the inclusion of the chicane and this added eight whole seconds to a lap time. The Argentinian 'Pampas Bull', Froilan Gonzales, with the Thin Wall Ferrari, was the new record holder at around 90 m.p.h.

Parnell (BRM), Ken Wharton (BRM), Hawthorn (Thin Wall Ferrari), Moss (Maserati), Tony Brooks (Vanwall), and Moss (Cooper) and Hawthorn (Ferrari), together on the same day, all raised the record progressively without reaching Farina's pre-chicane time of 1 minute 28 seconds and it was not until 1960 that Moss, with Rob Walker's Cooper-Climax, which was eventually vanquished by Innes Ireland in the new rear-engined Lotus 18, blasted the old speed with a lap in 1 minute 24.6 seconds, 102.13 m.p.h.—the first time that Goodwood had been lapped in a race at over the ton.

Despite the reduction in Formula 1 engine capacity from 2½ to 1½ litres in 1961, it was not long before the lap record speed went up again and it was with that fateful drive of Easter Monday, 1962, that Moss in the Lotus reached the new height of 105.37 m.p.h., in conjunction with the Lola of John Surtees.

In 1964, Graham Hill (BRM) raised it to 106.67 m.p.h. in a race won by Jim Clark's Lotus and the following year the record reached its official all-time high with Clark (Lotus) and Jackie Stewart (BRM) sharing it at 1 minute 20.4 seconds, 107.46 m.p.h.

So, the new generation of drivers were very much in command, most of them having cut their racing teeth on the Sussex track, with its sweeping double-radius bends, smooth and predictable surface and wide run-off of grass. Relatively speaking, it was so safe to spin at Goodwood that many drivers were lulled into a false sense of security. The BARC, ever gluttons for punishment from within the correspondence columns, introduced a 'no-spinning' rule at Club meetings, whereby a competitor who spun had a penalty of one minute added to his race time.

One of the more memorable Club battles was the first Formula Junior race of 1960, when the field included John Surtees, entered in a Cooper by Ken Tyrrell and having his first-ever car race. A multi-world champion of motor cycles, he needed to compete in a Club meeting to gain a fully international competition licence for car racing. Opposing him were Jim Clark and Trevor Taylor in the works Lotus cars. What a race! Eventually, leader Surtees paused momentarily when about to lap a back marker, Clark snatched the lead and they finished Clark-Surtees-Taylor. In a remarkably short time, all three were Grand Prix drivers.

With the '60s, Goodwood went into a decline.

The chicane at Goodwood was intended to be a hazard not a car-basher and the solid-looking wall was mostly wooden advertisement hoardings on castors—but on the apex of the corner it was solid brick (above). Goodwood's last big race (below) with Hill (Cooper) ahead of Clark (Lotus) and Rindt (Brabham) on Easter Monday, 1966.

There was a tightening of purse strings and a slackening of the pace of improvements.

As this decline coincided with a drastic change in the whole pattern of car racing, the end was in sight. Although there had, in some seasons, been as many as ten meetings at Goodwood, mostly there were no more than eight. Now, eight races in one year was no longer enough to make sufficient money to sustain an international motor-racing circuit when only one of those meetings (Goodwood's traditional Easter Monday date) was attracting a full-scale crowd.

Two factors prevented the obvious step of running more meetings. One was the insistence that Sunday racing was out. Rightly or wrongly, that was the circuit's attitude, backed up by the knowledge that, because of noise, motor racing had never been very popular with the immediate local residents. Although they were invisible from the track, there were quite a number of houses within earshot.

Secondly, there was the growing preoccupation by the Goodwood management with the horse-racing up on the hill, so that eventually car meetings were not staged after the beginning of July, nor could the BARC hire the circuit for the club to do it all alone. In any case, Saturday afternoon club meetings were so poorly supported by spectators in the mid-'60s that there can have been no encouragement to hold more of them.

The final straw was the decision, largely that of the Duke of Richmond and Gordon himself, that in the interests of spectator safety, the 1966-onwards 3-litre Grand Prix cars could not be raced at Goodwood. In 1966 itself, this was no problem. Nobody involved wanted to stake all in getting a representative field of 3-litre cars in a non-championship event in April, so Goodwood's Easter International was for the 1-litre Formula 2 models. Remarkably quick they were, too, with Denny Hulme setting a class lap record at a rousing 105 m.p.h., but the public wasn't impressed.

The BARC decided that it could not accept a future in which its biggest and best meeting of the year could never include a Formula 1 race, so it took its Easter International to Silverstone for 1967 (ironically, though, the club has not staged Formula 1 since leaving Goodwood). Without an international on Easter Monday, Goodwood was certainly not a viable proposition.

The last Goodwood race meeting was held on Saturday, 2 July, 1966 and pretty quiet it was. Most of the BARC were at the much bigger meeting which the club was also organising at Crystal Palace.

The course is still in good condition to this day and now the really fast boys lap it in under 70 seconds. Without the chicane they would probably get round in about 65 seconds (133 m.p.h.!). It is still one of the most-used British circuits for Formula 1 testing and with its flying and various other operations it is by no means dormant.

To most people, it is just a happy memory but British motor racing owes a lot to 'Glorious Goodwood'.

Jochen Rindt—
A Coming Champion?

JOCHEN RINDT, No. 1 driver in the Lotus works team, was brought up in Austria but was, in fact, born in Germany of a German father and Austrian mother. Both parents were killed in an air-raid in 1943 and Jochen was taken care of by his maternal grandparents who lived at Gratz. After a bright start in rallies and saloon car races, he turned to single-seaters at the age of 21 (in 1963) with a Formula Junior Cooper. Won a Formula 2 race at Crystal Palace in 1964, was offered a Formula 1 drive by Rob Walker and got a three-year contract with Cooper-Maserati. Won 1965 Le Mans and after a season with Brabham, joined Lotus in 1969. Now he is tipped as a coming champion—and is the man world champion Jackie Stewart regards as his biggest danger.

Rindt in the Ferrari in which, with Masten Gregory, he won the Le Mans 24-Hour Race of 1965.

Rindt (right) now lives at Geneva (a near-neighbour is Jackie Stewart) with his wife, Nina, and their young daughter. His recreations include ski-ing, yachting and tennis. So far, his Grand Prix racing luck has been patchy. Cooper-Maserati was a combination which never hit the top and the year Rindt raced for the Brabham team was an off one for 'Black Jack'. Even in 1969, there was a little uncertainty since Lotus appeared to have two No. 1 drivers, Rindt and the then champion, Graham Hill. In 1970, as undisputed No. 1 for Lotus, Rindt may at last fulfil the promise recognised by all the experts. Jochen (below), in a Gold Leaf Team Lotus during the 1969 Race of Champions at Brands Hatch in which he set up a record lap of 109.91 m.p.h.

Rindt adjusts his face-mask (above) whilst a Firestone mechanic checks his tyres before the RAC British Grand Prix at Silverstone. Rindt leads Stewart (below). The two had a fantastic battle before Jochen was forced to drop back, eventually being placed fourth behind Stewart, Ickx and McLaren.

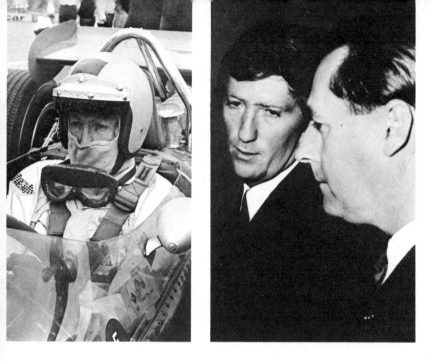

Three faces of a man: (above, left) Jochen Rindt at the wheel of his Lotus; (above, right) with three-times world champion, Jack Brabham, in 1967; and (below) with his wife Nina, when they were in the Argentine for the 1968 Temporada series, in which Jochen was placed second overall.

Jochen Rindt is a man of many parts: above, with the Gurney team at Indianapolis in 1967. Dan Gurney himself is third from the left, standing at the back. Below: a view of the 1968 Jochen Rindt Racing Car Show in Vienna. Rindt has organised this show every year since 1965, on behalf of the Austrian Automobile Club.

THE ENGINE MAN
by buzz barre

ON the circuit, new Grand Prix cars were being tested. A 'whirly-bird', carrying a BBC cameraman, circled above. But for a solid-looking, clean-shaven citizen on the ground, his fair 'going-on-grey' hair ruffled by the keen Northants wind, there were other problems.

Keith Duckworth had been awarded the Dewar Trophy by the Royal Automobile Club 'for the design of the Ford Formula One engine which has retained the supremacy of British engineering in Grand Prix racing' and had learned with horror that he was to receive the award at a formal black

tie and tuxedo dinner at RAC headquarters. The prospect of dinner didn't worry Keith—the thought of making a speech did.

So now, as Jackie Stewart and Chris Amon 'did their thing' on the Silverstone circuit, Duckworth sought the advice of a couple of RAC officials on what was expected of him when he received the trophy.

Said one, 'Don't worry, just a couple of words will do.'

'Like "thank you"?' asked Keith hopefully.

In the event he did much better than that but it

is no secret to anyone who knows him that Master Duckworth is far happier at a drawing-board than delivering orations to assembled throngs.

The Dewar Trophy which might well be termed Britain's premier automotive award is a unique distinction and fitting recognition of Duckworth's work. One hesitates to say it crowns his achievements since at 37 this remarkable chap still has plenty of time to surprise the twin worlds of engineering and car racing.

Nevertheless, the award adds the name of this modest Lancastrian—born Blackburn, 1933—to a roll call of the great. First presented in 1906, it went to the Dennis firm (of fire engine fame) when one of their cars covered the then remarkable distance of 4,000 miles. Rolls-Royce were next—going 11,000 miles better. Then came one of the many car import firms which were proliferating at the time, the Anglo-American Motor Car Company which, with that dear old motoring pioneer Fred Bennett as the moving spirit, conducted a test to demonstrate how all parts on Cadillac cars were standard and interchangeable, three cars being dismantled, the parts mixed up and the cars rebuilt again. In a day and age when most cars were 'one offs' this was something quite remarkable.

The following year—1909—Daimler took the award when one of their engines was run for 132 hours on the test bench, installed in a car and then did 2,000 miles on the Brooklands race track.

Racing motorist S. F. Edge was the next recipient, driving a Napier from London to Edinburgh and back in top gear. Thomas transmissions then achieved recognition, a car so equipped covering 2,000 miles while a lorry managed London to Edinburgh and back—not in top gear.

There was a gap of a year then Fred Bennett won again with another demonstration of the prowess of Cadillac cars. Fred was a remarkable man who, in his eighties, still competed regularly in the London to Brighton veteran car run.

There was time for one more winner before the war clouds loomed over Europe. The National Steam Company received the trophy in 1914 for a fuel consumption test on a lorry designed to run on coke.

In 1920, the Dewar came back into circulation and was won by National Benzole for a 10,000 miles trial. Thornycroft took it the following year with their BT-type lorry and then came Armstrong-Siddeley with another 10,000 miles trial. The Rapson Tyre and Jack Company came next with a design for cord tyres and then Rovers managed to get one of their cars up a Welsh mountain and back no less than 50 times on the trot. In 1926 and 1929, an outstanding woman motorist, Violette Cordery, was awarded the trophy for outstanding achievements with Invicta cars and in between— in 1928—C. B. Wardman won it for a trial with a Mercedes Benz heavy lorry.

After 1929, the award was allowed to lapse for a number of years, apparently because it was thought that the great pioneering days of motoring were over and there could be nothing new under the sun —or more correctly for Great Britain, the rain.

But in 1950, the RAC thought the time ripe to revive the award and it went in that year to Rovers again but this time for the design and development of the gas turbine car. Jaguars, by putting Britain on the map with successes in four international events including Le Mans, won it in 1951 and Sunbeam-Talbot the following year for winning the Alpine Rally.

Then, as British successes began to stockpile, it became difficult to single out individual achievements one from the other and for five years the Trophy was not awarded. Then in 1957, the work of Dunlops, both in developing disc brakes and in developing tyres for the record-breaking MGs, was appropriately recognised.

The 1958 winner was Tony Vandervell for the design, development and production of the Vanwall car and in 1959, BMC and Alec Issigonis received it for 'advanced development in automobile design as exemplified by the Morris Mini-Minor and Austin Seven.' In recent years, the Technical and Engineering Committee which advises the RAC on the award, has found it increasingly difficult to nominate worthy winners with the result that Duckworth's award was only the third made in the past eleven years.

In 1963, Coventry-Climax Engines won it for

...ham Hill (Campbell Trophy), Keith Duckworth ...ewar) and Jackie Stewart (Hawthorn) receive their ...ards at the RAC.

physics and chemistry. He went into the RAF for his National Service but, of all things, damaged a leg in a Rugby match and after a long spell in hospital, was discharged from the Service. In fact, at this stage of his life, things were not going too smoothly. He signed on as an engineering student at the Imperial College in South Kensington but what should have been a three-year course turned into four since an attack of glandular fever caused him to miss his second-year exams.

In 1955, still at college, he bought a Mk VI Lotus—in kit form as did most young enthusiasts —and installed an 1100 .cc Climax engine. But it didn't take Keith long to discover that he wasn't cut out to be a racing driver. In only his third race he went through the chicane at Goodwood instead of round it and that was that.

One gets the feeling that he doesn't particularly regret it. He's been quoted as saying, 'Some people are natural drivers; and some become half-proficient by practising a great deal. I definitely fell into the latter category and that didn't strike me as reasonable.'

But the venture was to have a significant affect on his career. It was his first association, however indirect, with Lotus and in one of his summer vacations he got a job at the factory which was then at Hornsey, North London. Among his work-mates was one Graham Hill. So, when he left college in 1957, he joined Lotus full-time as a development engineer.

He didn't stay long. Ten months in fact. Some men leave jobs for more money elsewhere or because they can't stand the sight of the foreman. Duckworth, typically, left Lotus because of a disagreement over a technical problem concerning gear-boxes.

But during that ten months, Keith had struck up a firm friendship with another Lotus engineer, Mike Costin. They decided to form Cosworth Engineering together and in 1958 the new enterprise came into being. Keith was to work at it full-time with Mike giving as much time as his job with Lotus would allow.

But Lotus boss, Colin Chapman, about this time asked Costin on to the board of Lotus Cars and at

an achievement now paralleled by Keith—'the design, development and production of engines which brought British cars to the forefront of Grand Prix racing.' And the only other 'modern' winner has been the Motor Industry Research Association —in 1967.

So Duckworth can be truly proud of having his name on that particular roll of honour although, as he himself has been quick to point out, he is by no means a one man band. Three other men, Mike Costin, Bill Brown and Benny Rood, have played important roles in the Duckworth story which began. . . .

. . . as the son of an engineer who owned a Blackburn weaving-shed. Although Keith's father died when Keith was 12, he had already implanted in his son a love of engineering and the correct use of tools. Both, in fact, were enthusiastic model-makers and while father was busy with ships, son was at work on aircraft, progressing from balsa wood and elastic bands to radio-controlled models.

Keith spent nine years as a boarder at Giggleswick School, Settle, Yorkshire, passed his School Certificate and went on to take 'A' levels in maths,

Keith Duckworth (right) with Harley Copp, of Fords, examining a Lotus-Ford. A shot from a Ford film, 'Nine Days In Summer'.

ham Hill leads Jean-Pierre Beltoise (Matra) on his
to his fifth victory in the Monaco Grand Prix, a feat
h earned him the RAC's Campbell Memorial Trophy.

the same time decreed that all directors were expected to devote all their time to Lotus.

So, for three years, the 'worth' part of the new organisation worked without the 'Cos'.

Duckworth plodded ahead working on other people's engines and suspensions, first from a garage in West London then from stables at Friern Barnet, Middlesex. Later he moved to a former Lotus workshop at Edmonton and then in 1964 to Northampton where the firm is still comfortably installed.

Back at the Lotus factory, Costin was responsible for the Lotus Formula Junior car and, meanwhile, Duckworth decided to produce a Formula Junior engine. Having surveyed the field, he decided on a Ford 105E engine (which powered the successful Anglias) as a basis and got down to work.

Team Lotus decided to buy all their Formula Junior engines from Duckworth and three very successful years followed, inevitably attracting attention from Fords. The start of the Duckworth-Ford association was modest, Ford offering what Duckworth called a 'token payment' towards the development of a new engine for Formula Two.

But it heralded bigger things. They were triggered off by the 1965 introduction of a three-litre limit for Formula One and the withdrawal of Coventry-Climax from motor racing. Climax had powered many of the most successful Grand Prix cars, including Cooper and Lotus, and Colin Chapman was rather desperate. He did not want to use BRM engines and he tried to persuade Duckworth to design an engine. There was one major snag—the design and development of Grand Prix engines costs money. A fairy godmother was required —and one was forthcoming in the un-fairy-like guise of the Ford Motor Company.

The rest of the story is motor-racing history. The Cosworth Ford engine won 15 times in its first 21 starts. In the 1968 World Championship series it won all but one race—the exception being the French Grand Prix won by Jacky Ickx in a Ferrari. In the 1969 series that slight omission was remedied and Cosworth Fords were fitted to the winners of every single one of the 11 Grands Prix. There were six wins for Matra-Ford, two apiece for

Brabham-Ford and Lotus-Ford and one for McLaren-Ford. In fact, these remarkable engines filled the first six places in every World Championship race with the exception of a fifth place for BRM in Spain, a third for Ferrari in Holland, sixth for Ferrari in Italy, third for BRM and fifth for Ferrari in the United States and sixth for BRM in Canada.

The man who designed those engines seems untouched by success unless one counts the Brantley Helicopter which he now uses to get from place to place. But he was happy when the plant moved to Northampton since he's never liked London, regarding it as far too big a place.

Now he and the family live four miles outside the town and when Keith isn't at the factory—which is often—he is to be found poring over the drawing board which was almost the first item of furniture installed in the new house.

Very happily married, Keith has a son and a daughter but is no advocate of the 'permissive society'. There has to be discipline, he believes, 'people need to jump'. Certainly, he doesn't seem a man to suffer fools gladly despite his mild manner.

The story is told of one individual who told Keith that a certain component had been designed by a computer. Duckworth exploded. 'What a fatuous idea,' he said, 'computers cannot think, they cannot design.'

At home in Northampton, Keith discusses one of life's little problems with Mrs Duckworth. Junior, however, seems much more interested in what the photographer is getting up to.

What does the future hold for Duckworth? He talks vaguely of being interested in building helicopters but hastens to add that the factory has to earn money to keep going. And earning money means building racing engines.

At the 1969 RAC British Grand Prix at Silverstone, there were expectations of the first complete car to appear from Cosworth but although the car duly made a public appearance, a great many problems manifested themselves.

A four-wheel drive, the Cosworth was designed by former McLaren backroom boy, Robin Herd, before he left to join the new March project. One of the problems was the tremendous physical effort required from the driver to get a four-wheel-drive car fitted with wide tyres around a track. It wasn't a problem peculiar to Cosworth, of course, Matra, Lotus and McLaren all experienced the same difficulty with their four-wheel-drive ventures. But it was a problem which, as Duckworth says, 'we should

have thought about before the car set a wheel on a track.'

It was a problem which Matra solved in rather drastic fashion for the Mexican Grand Prix. They disconnected the drive to the front wheels which, of course, converted the car back to two-wheel-drive and rather defeated the object of the whole exercise. The McLaren and Cosworth cars were withdrawn, the Cosworth without actually racing.

It is unlikely that Duckworth will give up on the idea although everyone else seems to have put four-wheel-drive back in the filing-cabinet and lost the key. But if there is to be a future for this type of car in racing then Duckworth appears to be the man most likely to solve the mystery and unlock the cabinet again. Despite the departure of Herd for March, Duckworth is still nibbling away and has already devised some modifications. The rest is in the future.

Meanwhile, Cosworth are busy on Formula

Three engines for the new formula which comes in in 1971. The world of motor racing is not likely to neglect the talents of a man who, more than any other in the history of the sport, has put his imprint on it. The domination achieved by his engines is unsurpassed and one probably has to go back to the colossal string of victories run up by Bugatti in the '20s and '30s to find a situation where the brain-children of one mind have accomplished so much.

Meantime, it was fitting that on the night when Britain's premier motoring organisation honoured Keith Duckworth with the Dewar Trophy, he was flanked by two of the drivers who shared in his success and drove Ford-powered cars, Graham Hill and Jackie Stewart.

World Champion Stewart received the Hawthorn Memorial Trophy as 'the British or Commonwealth driver placed highest in the World Championship.' You can't be much higher than first. And Hill took the Campbell Trophy for 'the outstanding performance by the British driver of a British car in any form of motor competition during the calendar year—winning the Monaco Grand Prix for the fifth time.' It was untrue, they said, that if Hill won the race for a sixth time, Prince Rainier would present him with the Casino.

But both Stewart and Hill agreed that it was high old time that Duckworth, the man who made it possible for them to be world champions, shared the limelight.

Another shot from 'Nine Days In Summer'. Graham Hill talks to Keith Duckworth before a race. Duckworth never misses a race in which the Formula One engines are involved—his way of checking that theory becomes practice.

FORMULA
5000

By Alan Brinton

Alan Brinton, motor-racing correspondent of the Observer, is one of Europe's most informed commentators on the motor-racing scene. Intimately connected with the new Formula 5000 since its conception, no one is better able to discuss the prospects for Europe's equivalent of America's Formula A. As Formula 5000 battles for existence in its second season, the question is: will it be a smash hit or, as less cultured theatre critics were wont to say, stink the place out?

THE birth of a new racing formula is always difficult. There are always those critics who say it isn't needed, others who declare that it will cut across current formulas, and still more who forecast that it cannot work.

It was like that with Formula 5000, which made its public début at Oulton Park on Good Friday, 1969. There were many sceptics before, and indeed after, that race, and in fact there *were* some problems for Formula 5000 race organisers during the season. But by the time the 12-event Guards Formula 5000 Championship finished with a race at Brands Hatch on September 28 there was little doubt that it had caught the affection not only of spectators but also of entrants.

It wasn't Grand Prix. For one thing, the races were shorter, and the Formula 5000 cars were not quite as fast as Formula 1. The really big names were lacking, too, because of an insistence that graded drivers could not take part. Some of the Formula 5000 cars which formed up on the grids were poorly prepared, and several proved fragile.

Yet despite this, the new formula provided the racegoer with fast, noisy, and at times exciting battles, the big names were not really missed, and as the season progressed the percentage of finishers improved.

And by the end of the season everyone was sufficiently encouraged to plan a far more ambitious Formula 5000 programme for 1970. The dozen-strong championship of 1969 grew into a far more ambitious series of 21 qualifying rounds for the Guards Formula 5000 Championship, with races in nine different countries. And more entrants and more constructors came in to swell the grids, helped no doubt by the decision that the formula was to be given trade support.

But what is Formula 5000 all about? Why was it called into being? Who was behind it?

Well, it was the brainchild of two of Britain's most experienced and go-ahead race promoters—John Webb, head of Motor Circuit Developments (who own most of Britain's major circuits, including Brands Hatch), and Nick Syrett, executive director of the British Racing and Sports Car Club. They were looking for a really quick and spectacular and noisy form of single-seater racing which could not cost as much as Formula 1 to run, to provide promising drivers with a chance of showing their skills, and give spectators good value for the money they paid at the turnstiles.

During 1968 the Americans had thought up Formula A, for single-seaters powered by 5 litre production-based push-rod V8 engines, and profit-

ing from this experience Webb and Syrett devised a parallel formula for Europe, differing only in detail from Formula A but giving it the title of Formula 5000 (for 5,000 c.c.) as being far more realistic and descriptive to European eyes.

In outline, Formula 5000 was for single-seater cars with 5 litre American V8 engines which could be 'breathed-on' quite considerably to give lots of power, with a minimum weight of 1,250 lbs. (For the first season, to ensure the grids were fairly full, cars weighing a minimum of 950 lbs using 2 litre 'pure' racing engines were also allowed.) The favourite power unit was developed from the Chevrolet Camaro Z28 engine, though one or two entrants used the V8 Ford 289 unit on the score of better reliability (though it was something like 100 brake horsepower down on the better Chevvys). These big engines gave a lot of power—around 420–430 b.h.p. for the Chevvy engines using carburettors, and a claimed 480 b.h.p. for the special fuel-injected engines used by the championship winner Peter Gethin. (For the 1970 season fuel injection was banned, and everyone was pleased since it meant a saving of several hundred pounds per engine.)

The most popular car during the first season of Formula 5000 was the Lola T142, a simple but

The eventual winner, Mike Hailwood, heads the parade prior to the start of a Formula 5000 race at Brands Hatch.

somewhat bulky spaceframe design that was a revised version of the T140 which Lola had produced the year before for Formula A. This was not the most competitive car in the series, but since it was based on Lola's T70 sports car it had the advantage of being reasonably cheap, and indeed Lola T142s filled most of the top places in the championship, apart from the first-place McLaren M10A and the runner-up TS5.

While the Lola was a space-framer, the McLaren M10A was a monocoque, based on the Formula 1 McLaren M7A. It was more sophisticated than the Lola, and several were sold in the United States, but in fact only one example appeared in Europe in 1969 . . . and took the Guards title.

John Surtees, former holder of the driver's world championship, saw Formula 5000 as a good stepping-

off platform for his plan to become one of the growing ranks of driver-constructors, and from his factory at Slough came the TS5, designed by Len Terry (responsible for many famous racing cars, including the Lotus 38 which gave Jim Clark victory in the Indianapolis 500 Miles in 1965). Like the McLaren, the TS5 was a monocoque, and it fairly soon became a formidable competitor after early teething troubles were overcome.

These, then, were the major contenders during Formula 5000's first season. What about the drivers? Since graded drivers were not allowed in the formula, it attracted a bunch of men of lesser driving stature than the Grand Prix stars, young men with the urge to get an apprenticeship with power under their right foot, established drivers who couldn't break through into Formula 1 (often for the simple basic

fact that there aren't enough Grand Prix cars to go round), and a bevy of chaps who simply wanted to enjoy themselves.

Indeed, if one feature dominated the first season of Formula 5000 it was that everyone had a thoroughly good time. There was a fine camaraderie among the pilots, which included some bright and breezy characters; so much so that some observers said it reminded them of those rather freer days in Grand Prix when fellows like Mike Hawthorn, Stirling Moss and Peter Collins seemed to race perhaps more for the enjoyment than the money.

I recall several years ago how, after the French Grand Prix at Reims, John Cooper was suddenly discovered conducting a full orchestra in the town hall during the prize-giving, to the encouraging cheers of the Grand Prix 'circus'. There was a rather similar mood about the post-race party staged in a nearby hotel after the final 1969 Formula 5000 championship battle at Brands Hatch. It was quite tremendous fun, with Mike Hailwood, the several times motorcycle world champion, and Ulf Norinder, a rich and bearded Swede, vying with one another at a couple of microphones with their interpretation of 'When

Former world champ, John Surtees, here in reflective mood, is emerging as a leading F5000 manufacturer.

the Saints go marching in' while Chris Barber and his boys blew themselves silly in an effort to keep up with them.

There was this great spirit throughout the season. Entrants swopped bits if they were in trouble, mechanics helped out a rival team, and there was one occasion when a competitor with engine problems was able to borrow a power unit which Ulf Norinder had flown over specially from Sweden. It was all good sporting stuff. When the flag dropped everyone did their damnedest, but off the circuit everyone was the best of pals.

The driver who came out on top, and took the Guards Formula 5000 Championship in dramatic fashion in the last qualifying event, was little Peter Gethin, only five feet seven inches tall and the son of Ken Gethin, who used to be one of Britain's best

flat race jockeys before he became a trainer. Until Formula 5000 came along, Peter's progress had been soured by the most awful history of bad luck; he was clearly above average in Formula 3, but so often he was let down by mechanical misfortune. But Formula 5000 gave him just the opportunity for which he had been hankering, and with the McLaren M10A which the Church Farm Racing Team were running on behalf of the works he probably had the best machine on the grid. Good preparation paid high dividends, and Peter set off in fine style to win the first four races in succession (though he had to work very hard in the fourth race at Mallory Park to fight off a very determined David Hobbs in one of the works TS5s).

After that, Peter's luck failed him at Silverstone in June, when he had to retire, and then he missed

On one of Europe's most delightful circuits, Oulton Park, Mike Walker's Lola stays ahead of Italy's Andrea de Adamich. Walker won a 1969 F5000 Championship race at Oulton Park and also took the chequered flag first at Silverstone.

the next four qualifiers through dashing off to the United States to take part in Formula A races with the M10A. By now, his early-season lead was being cut back, by Keith Holland, in Alan Fraser's Lola T142, and Trevor Taylor, who had taken over David Hobbs' place in the Team Surtees line-up. In fact, Peter failed to win any more Formula 5000 races, but fourth place overall at Hockenheim, in Germany, gave him points that were to land him the Guards title.

Trevor Taylor didn't come into the formula until it was well under way, but became a regular TS5 driver at the half-way stage in the championship. At one time, Trevor used to be in the Lotus GP team

Brands Hatch in late September, was marred by an incident that put both top contenders out of action. They were having a splendid tussle, with Trevor in the lead, when they both left the circuit through a misunderstanding when trying to overtake a tail-ender.

So Peter became Guards champion, and Trevor had to be satisfied with second place (though he firmly established himself back as a top driver to be reckoned with).

Third place in the championship went to Mike 'the Bike' Hailwood, who some time earlier had had a go at Grand Prix racing but had pulled out after disappointments through lack of competitive

along with Jim Clark, but had gradually faded out of the picture after a series of unfortunate accidents, and later almost gave up racing altogether when plagued with back trouble. But Formula 5000 brought him back with a vengeance; he equalled Peter Gethin's performance by winning four qualifying races in a row. Then in the last two races, at Oulton Park and Brands Hatch, neither he nor Peter managed to finish, and the championship went to Peter.

It was such a shame that the final decider, at

machinery. For Formula 5000, Mike had the Lola T142 which the works were using as a development car, sponsored by Jackie Epstein and Nick Cuthbert. The Lola was certainly more of a handful than the rival McLaren and TS5s, and Mike had to work hard to provide them with competition. The Lola gradually got better as the season progressed, and Mike clearly enjoyed throwing it around, but it was not until half-way through the series that his luck turned when, at Mondello Park, in Ireland, he came second overall in spite of being almost roasted

Trevor Taylor (TS5), F5000 victor at Koksijde, Zandvoort, Snetterton and Hockenheim, was edged out for the title by Pete Gethin.

in the cockpit. In later races he picked up a third place and a couple of seconds and then, in that last race at Brands Hatch, he took the chequered flag at last and snatched third place in the championship from Keith Holland.

Keith Holland also had a Lola T142, and displayed an amazing consistency with it (after being thrown in at the deep end for the opening race following a road accident which put Alan Fraser's nominated driver, Tony Lanfranchi, out of action). Keith, who hails from Maidstone, never looked like winning any of the races, but concentrated successfully on coming home with the car in one piece, a tactic that paid off with only one retirement and a score that included one second place and no less than five thirds.

Another driver who thoroughly enjoyed the

Formula 5000 taste of power was Alan Rollinson, a star of Formula 3 who put the cat among the 5 litre pigeons with a second and third place at Silverstone and Mondello Park with a Formula 2 Brabham, and then took over Doug Hardwick's Lola T142 to demonstrate that he knew how to adapt himself to 400 horsepower-plus. In his very first outing with the Lola, Alan scored a second place at Koksijde, in Belgium, and by finishing with a brace of seconds in the final two races he landed fifth place in the championship.

The best example of how Formula 5000 can help a young man with skill and ambition was Mike Walker, from the Midlands, who started his competition career in 1964 with a venerable 500 c.c. Kieft. He had a miserable season during 1968 when everything went wrong, and then out of the blue

Almost wheel-to-wheel in a Formula 5000 Guards Championship Race at Brands Hatch.

came the offer of a Lola T142 belonging to Alan McKechnie. His bad luck didn't entirely desert him, for the car was continually plagued by overheating problems, but he drove immaculately and by the end of the season he had notched a couple of Formula 5000 victories, at Silverstone in June and at Oulton Park in September, to take sixth place in the championship. His performances during the season attracted the attention of many experts, and it was capped by the premier prize in the annual Grovewood Motor Racing Awards.

Mike Walker is a quiet, shy person (though this hides a very determined approach to motor racing) but Ulf Norinder, who finished just behind him in the championship, is the true extrovert. Ulf drove yet another Lola T142, and this huge man clearly enjoyed every minute of his Formula 5000 races. It was something of a surprise to British racegoers to learn that Ulf first raced in 1954 and that motor racing had been his main activity for more than ten years. But in Formula 5000 he found the type of racing which suited his style and personality. At every circuit he was the idol, with his dashing style of dressing and his equally dashing driving. He was often in trouble, and was involved in many a hair-raising incident (though he declared, 'A lot of times I've spun just for the hell of it') but he came through it all with a broad smile, and by the end of the season was convinced that there was no better brand of racing than Formula 5000.

Along with David Hobbs, who scored a win and a couple of seconds before he went off to America, these were the leading Formula 5000 drivers of that first year, but many other drivers were involved during the season, and several of them were sufficiently encouraged to make more ambitious plans.

As the season drew to a close it was clear that Formula 5000 had vindicated the promises and hopes of its promoters. It had had its problems and its critics (and some of them were justified), but it had won through, to give racing fans a taste of power and excitement and noise, and provide the racing scene with something new. Which was just what it set out to do.

TRIBUTE TO A RACER — PAUL HAWKINS

A GREAT cloud of black smoke spiralled up into the sunny blue sky. People stopped, turned, pointed . . . some started running, where to who knew? Suddenly the roar of engines died away. As if on a signal, even the chatter of conversation ceased and, for a few terrible moments there was a complete and awe-inspiring silence. It was almost as if someone had announced the end of the world and so delivering that final decision had stunned all listeners into silence.

In fact, it was the end of someone's world. For Australia's Paul Hawkins, round-the-world-traveller, racing driver, tough, extrovert and popular, had driven his last race and that cloud of smoke marked what remained of driver and car.

The scene was Oulton Park, the race the RAC's 34th International Tourist Trophy.

The TT, which had been in the doldrums these past few years, had attracted a good field of 31 cars, dominated by the big 5-litre Lolas, and, for once, there was a goodly number of leading sports car drivers on the grid.

Apart from Targa Florio winner, Hawkins, there was Jo Bonnier, Brian Redman, David Piper, Trevor Taylor, David Prophet, Mac Daghorn, Digby Martland, Richard Attwood, Jackie Oliver, John Miles and Charles Lucas.

And the race lived up to expectations. There was plenty of excitement from the start with Muller, driving the Bonnier car, taking an early lead hotly chased by Hawkins. Muller's surprising performance ended after an hour when the Lola spun into a fence and could not continue. A pit stop caused Hawkins to drop back but he began working his way through the field. By lap 74, despite another pit stop, he was in seventh place and going like fury. Then it happened.

From a marshal's post near Esso bend, the words gabbled over the 'phone: Hawkins had gone off, rebounded from post to tree and exploded in mid-air. The car might just as well have been a bomb—Hawkins never had a chance. Flaming fuel spilled across the track, the race was halted and awarded to the leader at the time, Trevor Taylor (Lola) with David Piper (Lola) second and John Miles (Lotus) third.

At an early stage of the TT, Goodwin (Chevron No. 14) is challenged by Hawkins (No. 37) (above). (Below) Goodwin's race is halted by engine trouble. He dives under the bonnet to investigate as David Piper (No. 38) sweeps by. The Chevron eventually rejoined the race after a stop of 32 minutes, stopped again five minutes later with fuel pump trouble but kept going to the end.

Trevor Taylor (above), declared winner of the TT when the race was halted after Hawkins' fatal accident. (Below) All that remained of Hawkins' Lola after the crash. Firemen and marshals clear up the debris after a tragedy which left everyone stunned.

YUMPING ROUND THE WORLD

RALLY drivers have a fine old name for that breath-taking moment when the car takes off and flies through the air with the greatest of ease. They call it 'yumping'.

But they do not have exclusive rights to the sport as some of the world's leading Grand Prix and sports car racing drivers demonstrate in the following pages.

Rolf Stommelen, Jean-Pierre Beltoise, Jackie Oliver, Ronnie Peterson and Jackie Ickx are amongst those who have experienced the delights (?) of 'yumping' as these International Motor Racing Book pictures show.

And there is more 'yumping' in the Ford motor racing film, 'Nine Days In Summer', another shot from which is shown above.

Readers will probably agree—it must be the finest close-up of a racing car wheel at full revs ever taken. The driver is the late Jim Clark.

Ron Ockenden was the photographer on the spot as the David Howes saloon went off in a big way at Silverstone throwing clouds and clods of earth high into the air. In the bottom picture, the debris (not to mention the PA system) has subsided. Officials rush to aid the driver who can be seen still seated at the wheel.

A Formula 2 Lotus takes off (above). Rolf Stommelen in the 1969 German Grand Prix at the Nürburgring. (Below) Anything Rolf can do, I can do better. Jean-Pierre Beltoise in the same race.

Caught at the moment of take-off: Sweden's Ronnie Peterson (March F3) at Cadwell Park. (Below) What sometimes happens when you come down. Jackie Oliver's BRM in sad and sorry state at Monaco where there were only seven finishers in 1969.

Keeping two wheels firmly (?) on the ground at the Cadwell Park International meeting: Nick Faure's Porsche 911 captured in mid-air by the camera of Nigel Snowdon.

Jackie Ickx (above) at the Nürburgring, an ideal circuit for those who want to indulge in the sport of 'yumping'; and (below) the kind of 'yump' drivers can do without—Pedro Rodriguez on collision course during the 1969 Spa Thousand Kilometres Race.

CHRIS AMON BY
CHRIS AMON

There are footballers who have never won a Cup Final medal, boxers who have never taken a title. New Zealand's Chris Amon would hate to be a Grand Prix driver who never won a Grand Prix. Yet, despite many successes in sports cars and other events, including Le Mans, ill-luck has dogged him in World Championship races. In 1970, he switched to the new March cars as No. I works driver after a period with Ferrari where he was often left to play a lone hand. Will his luck change?

117

Chris Amon and Mario Andretti before the start of the Monza 1000 Kilometres Race.

Chris Amon (above) in action at the Nürburgring during the 1000 Kilometres Race. First lap at Monaco (below) with Stewart leading from Amon, Beltoise, Hill, Siffert, Surtees and Brabham. One of the friendliest drivers in the 'big-time' (opposite), Chris talks with journalists before the start of the RAC British Grand Prix at Silverstone.

*I*N motor-racing circles, the winter months invariably bring a spate of rumours and speculation about the plans of drivers and teams for the following season. Far from being an exception, the winter of *1969–70* had more than its quota of such speculation, some of which centred around the head of Chris Amon. Amon who had written in International Motor Racing Book No. 2 'Then came the second big break of my career—Ferrari signed me for the *1967* racing season' was rumoured to be leaving the Italian firm. He agreed to talk to us about it and on the eve of the *1970* season tape-recorded some thoughts on both past and future . . .

Q. Who will you drive for in 1970 in (a) Grand Prix racing; and (b) sports car racing?

A. Certainly March for Formula 1 and 2 and probably for the Can-Am series also. But I shall also drive for Ferrari in some selected sports car races.

Q. What are your motor-racing ambitions in (a) the short-term; and (b) the long-term?

A. To win a Grand Prix. And to win the World

Championship and be successful in all forms of motor racing.

Q. Looking many years ahead, do you hope to stay in motor sport when your active driving career ends or do you have other plans?

A. That's a difficult one to answer at present as it depends on what happens in the immediate future. I doubt if I would do another Brabham or McLaren and become a car manufacturer.

119

Encouragement for aspiring photographers: this fine picture of Chris Amon at speed was taken from the public enclosures by International Motor Racing Book reader Roger Hall, of Eltham (London).

Distance gets foreshortened and the cars seem to be climbing over one another in this shot from the BOAC 500 at Brands Hatch with Chris Amon (Ferrari) in front of Germany's Rolf Stommelen (Porsche).

However, I wouldn't mind entering cars as a private team like Ken Tyrrell or Rob Walker. I will always try to be connected with the sport, although I am keen on flying which may take up more of my time in the distant future.

Q. What was the most exciting moment of your 1969 racing season?

A. Winning the Tasman Championship back home in New Zealand and Australia. I had four wins in the seven race series, including victory in both the New Zealand and the Australian Grand Prix, totalling 44 points against 30 for Jochen Rindt (Lotus-Ford) and 22 for Piers Courage (Brabham-Ford).

Q. What was the greatest disappointment of your 1969 racing season?

A. Not winning a Grand Prix. Particularly disappointing was breaking down in the Spanish Grand Prix when I had led for many laps after starting in the middle of the front row of the

grid with Rindt and Hill. They both had accidents and Jackie Stewart went on to win from Bruce McLaren.

Q. What has been the greatest moment of your racing career to date?

A. Without a doubt, the first time I drove a Formula 1 Ferrari at Monaco in 1967. It had always been one of my dreams to drive a Ferrari since my early teens.

Q. What was the most humorous incident that has ever occurred to you in motor racing?

A. On reflection, the 12-Hour Sports Car Race at Reims in 1964 when, with Jackie Stewart, I drove an old GTO Ferrari for Ulf Norrinder. After running for four hours I came into the pits for a fuel change and to change the disc pads. They were nowhere to be found. After searching we discovered that they were locked up in a car in the paddock and nobody had the keys of the car. They were eventually found and the pads were fitted, but we had had a delay of some 20 minutes which didn't help as we were having a lot of trouble starting the car. The next pit stop Jackie came in for a tyre change and again we couldn't find one of the spare wheels. After some delay it was discovered that the wheel had been in the boot of the Ferrari all the time. This incident would have made a very comic sketch for a show. However, we did finish the race well up, in spite of not being able to start the car very well because of a faulty solenoid. We also lost second and fourth gears.

Q. What has been the most dramatic incident you have been involved in?

A. My crash at Monza in '68. While lying second, the oil pipe connected to the hydraulic wing we were using fractured, spraying oil on to the left rear tyre. I spun going into the first Lesmo and hit the guard rail backwards. The guard rail bent and catapulted the car, somersault-ing three times, landing the car down a bank on an access road. This had been the first race I used safety belts, which saved me from injury.

Q. You are one of the few English-speaking drivers to have been a regular member of a foreign works team. Have you found this to present great difficulties? Are there misunderstandings over language?

A. Obviously the language difficulties can be a problem but generally speaking I was able to communicate with Dr Gozzi, Team Manager, and Mauro Forgheiri, the Chief Engineer, as they both spoke some English, and by the time I had been there a year, I was able to speak some Italian. Mauro Forgheiri has a deep appreciation of how to make a car work, there-fore easing communications between us. Just the same, there were numerous comic incidents with Ferrari, particularly pit stops on the long-distance races.

Q. Where are you now based? And how many

On the flat featureless landscape of Silverstone, Graham Hill, Chris Amon and Piers Courage play follow-my-leader.

miles do you cover each year: by road, by air, by ship?

A. Geneva. By road, 25,000 miles; by air, in excess of 100,000 miles.

Q. Who do you consider to be the outstanding drivers during the years you have been racing yourself?

A. Jim Clark and Stirling Moss. Although I competed with Stirling Moss at the beginning of my career it is difficult to compare the two as Moss retired from active racing after my second year in Europe, when I was not driving very competitive cars at the time. Although Clark was challenged in some races, he was generally completely dominant. I don't really think he needed to extend himself fully.

Q. Which car have you most enjoyed driving?

A. Formula 1 Ferrari, particularly in 1968, as they had a very good handling car although down in power compared with the Ford-engined cars. This good road holding made up for engine deficiency.

Q. Apart from the driver, which factors do you regard as most important for success in Grand Prix racing—tyres, engine, gearbox, braking, body and chassis design, driver comfort, team manager?

A. Tyres play an important part. The engine has been my biggest problem during the last three years. But the chassis is very important.

Q. Which circuit do you prefer to race on?

A. I haven't any special preference but I do dislike slipstreaming-type circuits.

Q. Bearing in mind that many readers of the International Motor Racing Book are youngsters, what advice would you give to the aspiring racing driver?

A. Difficult to advise, but I would have thought that taking a course at a racing school could be some benefit and competing in Formula Ford races.

Q. You drove to second place in the Sebring 12-Hour Race. What do you think of motor racing in the United States? And would you like to have a crack at the Indianapolis 500-Mile Race?

A. I like racing in America. I do more races there than anywhere else. Racing is growing very fast there and advancing faster than in Europe. I am driving at Indianapolis this year for the McLaren team.

Q. All sorts of stories have appeared in the motor racing press that you are going to drive for March, that you are not going to drive for March, you have quarrelled with Ferrari, you have not quarrelled with Ferrari and so on. What is the truth of the matter?

A. The truth is that I did not quarrel with Ferrari but after three years I decided it was time for a change. I am happy to say that I am keeping my association with them in sports cars. My three years with the Italian team were very interesting and enjoyable but naturally I was disappointed that I didn't win a Grand Prix with them.

Q. Why do you think so many New Zealand and Australian drivers have been prominent in motor racing in recent years whereas countries like France and Italy which have been in motor sport since the beginning have produced relatively few stars?

A. The main reason is that in New Zealand and Australia we have had to cope with inferior tracks and out-of-date machinery but at the same time we were given the opportunity to drive Formula 1 cars, although old ones, in races against top European drivers who came over once a year for the season. For instance, at the beginning of 1962 I drove at the New Zealand Grand Prix in a Maserati at the age of 17. By English standards I was a very inexperienced club driver, driving against Messrs Brabham, McLaren, Surtees, Bandini, etc., and thus able to learn a lot from these people. Aspiring drivers in Europe don't get the same opportunity. Certainly Italian drivers have a serious lack of good circuits to learn on and don't get the same chances as the English driver.

Another scene from the BOAC 500 at Brands Hatch (which in 1970 became the BOAC 1000 Kilometres as Britain began the process of going metric).

HOW THEY MADE OUT

REGULAR readers of International Motor Racing have frequently requested that each issue should include the principal results of the past season.

We have hesitated to do this since we have always tried to present a different slant on the exciting world of motor racing and there are other books on the market which concentrate on the statistical side of the sport.

However, readers continue to press for the inclusion of results and as, unhappily, one or two other regular publications have recently fallen by the wayside, International Motor Racing Book No. 4 includes results for the first time.

In the following pages will be found the outcome of most of the major races and championships with the emphasis, as you might expect, on the Grand Prix clashes for the World Championship. But we will welcome suggestions from readers on what results you would like to see included in future editions which we have not listed this time.

The Editor

Rico Steineman (right), team manager of the successful championship-winning Porsche team in 1969, holds out a pit signal during the 1000 Kilometres Race at Spa. No prizes for guessing that the letters refer to one, Joseph Siffert.

FORMULA 1—WORLD CHAMPIONSHIP

March 1—South African Grand Prix

80 laps of 2.55-mile Kyalami Circuit

1 J. Stewart (Matra-Ford), 1h. 50m. 39.1s., 110.62 m.p.h.
2 G. Hill (Lotus-Ford), 1h. 50m. 57.9s.
3 D. Hulme (McLaren-Ford), 1h. 51m. 10.9s.
4 J. Siffert (Lotus-Ford), 1h. 51m. 28.3s.
5 B. McLaren (McLaren-Ford), 79 laps
6 J.-P. Beltoise (Matra-Ford), 78 laps
Nine finishers
Record lap: Stewart, 1m. 21.6s., 112.50 m.p.h.

May 4—Spanish Grand Prix

90 laps of 2.36-mile Montjuich Circuit

1 J. Stewart (Matra-Ford MS80), 2h. 16m. 54.0s., 92.91 m.p.h.
2 B. McLaren (McLaren-Ford M7C), 88 laps
3 J.-P. Beltoise (Matra-Ford MS80), 87 laps
4 D. Hulme (McLaren-Ford M7A), 87 laps
5 J. Surtees (BRM P138), 84 laps
6 J. Ickx (Brabham-Ford BT26), 83 laps
Six finishers
Record lap: J. Rindt (Lotus-Ford 49B), 1m. 28.3s., 96.03 m.p.h.

May 18—Monaco Grand Prix

80 laps of 1.9-mile Monte-Carlo Circuit

1 G. Hill (Lotus-Ford), 1h. 56m. 59.4s., 80.171 m.p.h.
2 P. Courage (Brabham-Ford), 1h. 57m. 16.7s.
3 J. Siffert (Lotus-Ford), 1h. 57m. 34.0s.
4 R. Attwood (Lotus-Ford), 1h. 57m. 52.3s.

5 B. McLaren (McLaren-Ford), 79 laps
6 D. Hulme (McLaren-Ford), 79 laps
Seven finishers
Fastest lap: J. Stewart (Matra-Ford), 1m. 25.1s., 80.38 m.p.h.

June 21—Dutch Grand Prix

90 laps of 2.62-mile Zandvoort Circuit

1 J. Stewart (Matra-Ford MS80), 2h. 6m. 42.08s., 111.042 m.p.h.
2 J. Siffert (Lotus-Ford 49B), 2h. 7m. 6.6s.
3 C. Amon (Ferrari V12), 2h. 7m. 12.59s.
4 D. Hulme (McLaren-Ford M7A), 2h. 7m. 19.24s.
5 J. Ickx (Brabham-Ford), 2h. 7m. 19.75s.
6 J. Brabham (Brabham-Ford), 2h. 7m. 52.89s.
Ten finishers
Record lap: Stewart, 1m. 22.94s., 113.086 m.p.h.

July 6—French Grand Prix

38 laps of 5.05-mile Charade Circuit, Clermont Ferrand

1 J. Stewart (Matra-Ford MS80), 1h. 56m. 47.4s., 97.711 m.p.h.
2 J.-P. Beltoise (Matra-Ford MS80), 1h. 57m. 44.5s.
3 J. Ickx (Brabham-Ford BT26), 1h. 57m. 44.7s.
4 B. McLaren (McLaren-Ford M7C), 37 laps
5 V. Elford (McLaren-Ford M7B), 37 laps
6 G. Hill (Lotus-Ford 49B), 37 laps
Ten finishers
Fastest lap: Stewart, 3m. 02.7s., 99.124 m.p.h.

Mario Andretti at the wheel of the four-wheel-drive Lotus during the 1969 German Grand Prix.

July 19—RAC British Grand Prix

84 laps of 2.93-mile Silverstone Circuit

1 J. Stewart (Matra-Ford MS80), 1h. 55m. 55.6s., 127.25 m.p.h.
2 J. Ickx (Brabham-Ford BT26), 83 laps
3 B. McLaren (McLaren-Ford M7C), 83 laps
4 J. Rindt (Lotus-Ford 49B), 83 laps
5 P. Courage (Brabham-Ford BT26), 83 laps
6 V. Elford (McLaren-Ford M7B), 82 laps
Ten finishers
Fastest lap: Stewart, 1m. 21.3s., 129.61 m.p.h.

August 3—German Grand Prix

14 laps of 14.19-mile Nürburgring Circuit

1 J. Ickx (Brabham-Ford BT26), 1h. 49m. 5.4s., 108.428 m.p.h.
2 J. Stewart (Matra-Ford MS80), 1h. 50m. 53.1s.
3 B. McLaren (McLaren-Ford M7C), 1h. 53m. 17s.
4 G. Hill (Lotus-Ford 49B), 1h. 53m. 54.2s.
5 J. Siffert (Lotus-Ford 49B), 12 laps
6 J.-P. Beltoise (Matra-Ford MS80), 12 laps
Six finishers
Fastest lap: Ickx, 7. 43.8s., 110.134 m.p.h.

September 7—Italian Grand Prix

68 laps of 3.57-mile Monza Circuit

1 J. Stewart (Matra-Ford MS80), 1h. 39m. 11.26s., 146.97 m.p.h.
2 J. Rindt (Lotus-Ford 49B), 1h. 39m. 11.34s.
3 J.-P. Beltoise (Matra-Ford MS80), 1h. 39m. 11.43s.
4 B. McLaren (McLaren-Ford M7C), 1h. 39m. 11.45s.
5 P. Courage (Brabham-Ford BT26), 1h. 39m. 44.7s.
6 P. Rodriguez (Ferrari), 66 laps
Eleven finishers
Fastest lap: Beltoise, 1m. 25.2s., 150.97 m.p.h.

September 20—Canadian Grand Prix

90 laps of 2.49-mile Mosport Circuit

1 J. Ickx (Brabham-Ford BT26), 1h. 59m. 25.7s., 112.76 m.p.h.
2 J. Brabham (Brabham-Ford BT26), 2h. 0m. 11.9s.
3 J. Rindt (Lotus-Ford), 2h. 0m. 17.7s.
4 J.-P. Beltoise (Matra-Ford MS80), 89 laps
5 B. McLaren (McLaren-Ford M7C), 87 laps
6 J. Servoz Gavin (4-wheel-drive Matra-Ford), 84 laps
Eight finishers
Fastest lap: Ickx and Brabham, 1m. 18.1s., 114.78 m.p.h.

October 6—U.S. Grand Prix

108 laps of 2.3-mile Watkins Glen Circuit

1 J. Rindt (Lotus-Ford 49), 1h. 57m. 56.84s. 126.36 m.p.h.
2 P. Courage (Brabham-Ford BT26), 1h. 58m. 43.83s.
3 J. Surtees (BRM P139), 106 laps
4 J. Brabham (Brabham-Ford BT26), 106 laps
5 P. Rodriguez (Ferrari V12), 101 laps
6 S. Moser (Brabham-Ford BT24), 98 laps
Six finishers
Record lap: Rindt, 1m. 04.34s., 128.69 m.p.h.

October 19—Mexican Grand Prix

65 laps of 3.107-mile Parkland Circuit

1 D. Hulme (McLaren-Ford M7A), 1h. 54m. 8.8s., 106.9 m.p.h.
2 J. Ickx (Brabham-Ford BT26), 1h. 54m. 11.36s.
3 J. Brabham (Brabham-Ford BT26), 1h. 54m. 47.28s.
4 J. Stewart (Matra-Ford MS80), 1h. 54m. 55.84s.
5 J.-P. Beltoise (Matra-Ford MS80), 1h. 55m. 47.32s.
6 J. Oliver (BRM), 63 laps
Eleven finishers
Record lap: Ickx, 1m. 43.05s., 108.53 m.p.h.

Drivers' Championship

1 J. Stewart	63 pts		4 J. Rindt		22
2 J. Ickx	37		5 J.-P. Beltoise	21	
3 B. McLaren	26		6 D. Hulme		20

Manufacturers' Championship

1 Matra-Ford 66 pts   4 McLaren-Ford 38
2 Brabham-Ford 49
3 Lotus-Ford 47   5 {BRM / Ferrari} 7

OTHER FORMULA 1 RACES

March 16—'Daily Mail' Race of the Champions, Brands Hatch

1 J. Stewart (Matra-Ford MS80), 1h. 13m. 10.4s., 108.65 m.p.h. (record)
2 G. Hill (Lotus-Ford 49B)
3 D. Hulme (McLaren-Ford M7A)
Record lap: J. Rindt (Lotus-Ford 49B), 1m. 26.8s., 109.91 m.p.h.

March 30—'Daily Express' International Trophy, Silverstone

1 J. Brabham (Brabham-Ford BT26), 1h. 25m. 20.8s., 107.0 m.p.h.
2 J. Rindt (Lotus-Ford 49B)
3 J. Stewart (Matra-Ford MS80)
Fastest lap: Rindt, 1m. 30.6s., 116.3 m.p.h.

August 16—Guards International Gold Cup, Oulton Park

1 J. Ickx (Brabham-Ford BT26), 1h. 0m. 28.6s., 109.57 m.p.h.
2 J. Rindt (Lotus-Ford 49B)
3 A. de Adamich (F5000 Surtees-Chevrolet)
Record lap: J. Stewart (Matra-Ford MS80), 1m. 28.6s., 112.19 m.p.h.

TASMAN SERIES—1969

January 4—New Zealand Grand Prix, Puke-kohe, New Zealand

1 C. Amon (2.4 Ferrari V6), 57m. 55.4s., 105 m.p.h. (record)
2 J. Rindt (2.5 Lotus-Ford 49B)
3 P. Courage (2.5 Brabham-Ford BT24 V8)
Record lap: Rindt, 58.9s., 107.7 m.p.h.

January 11—Rothmans International, Levin, New Zealand

1 C. Amon (2.4 Ferrari V6), 50m. 8.8s., 88.7 m.p.h.
2 P. Courage (2.5 Brabham-Ford BT24 V8)
3 F. Gardner (2.5 Mildren Alfa Romeo V8)
Fastest lap: Rindt, (2.5 Lotus-Ford 49B), 45.7s., 92.56 m.p.h.

Crowded pit road at Silverstone during the RAC British Grand Prix meeting. Not much room for cars and drivers.

January 18—Lady Wigram Trophy, Christchurch, New Zealand

1 J. Rindt (2.5 Lotus-Ford 49B), 58m. 53.6s., 103.11 m.p.h. (record)
2 G. Hill (2.5 Lotus-Ford 49T)
3 C. Amon (2.4 Ferrari V6)
Record lap: Rindt and Amon, 1m. 18.8s., 105.08 m.p.h.

January 25—Rothmans Teetonga International, Invercargill, New Zealand

1 P. Courage (2.5 Brabham-Ford BT24 V8), 1h. 1m. 14.4s., 97.38 m.p.h.
2 G. Hill (2.5 Lotus-Ford 49T)
3 C. Amon (2.4 Ferrari V6)
Fastest lap: Courage, 58.0s., 99.39 m.p.h.

February 2—Australian Grand Prix, Lakeside

1 C. Amon (2.4 Ferrari V6), 1h. 0m. 12.8s., 100.18 m.p.h.
2 D. Bell (2.4 Ferrari V6)
3 L. Geoghegan (2.5 Lotus-Repco 39)
Record lap: Amon, 52.8s., 102.272 m.p.h.

February 9—Tasman International 100, Warwick Farm, Australia

1 J. Rindt (2.5 Lotus-Ford 49B), 1h. 18m. 12.8s., 77.73 m.p.h.
2 D. Bell (2.4 Ferrari V6)
3 F. Gardner (2.5 Mildren Alfa Romeo V8)
Fastest lap: G. Hill (2.5 Lotus-Ford 49T), 1m. 40.3s.

Night pit stop for the 1969 Le Mans winning GT40.

February 16—Sandown Park, Australia
1 C. Amon (2.4 Ferrari V6), 1h. 0m. 10.6s., 106.1 m.p.h. (record)
2 J. Rindt (2.5 Lotus-Ford 49B)
3 J. Brabham (2.5 Brabham-Repco BT31 V8)
Record lap: Amon, 64.5s., 107.6 m.p.h.

Tasman Championship Results
1 C. Amon   44 points
2 J. Rindt   30
3 P. Courage   22

SPORTS CAR CHAMPIONSHIP

February 1/2—Daytona 24-hour race
1 M. Donohue/C. Parsons (Lola-Chevrolet T70), 626 laps, 99.27 m.p.h.
2 L. Motschenbacher/E. Leslie (Lola-Chevrolet)
3 J. Ward/J. Titus (Pontiac Firebird)

March 22—Sebring 12-hour race
1 J. Ickx/J. Oliver (Ford GT40), 239 laps
2 M. Andretti/C. Amon (Ferrari 312P)
3 K. Ahrens/J. Buzzetta (Porsche 908)

April 13—BOAC 500, Brands Hatch
1 J. Siffert/B. Redman (Porsche 908), 227 laps, 100.22 m.p.h.
2 V. Elford/R. Attwood (Porsche 908)
3 G. Mitter/U. Schutz (Porsche 908)

April 25—Monza 1,000 km.
1 J. Siffert/B. Redman (Porsche 908), 4h. 53m. 41.2s., 128.96 m.p.h.
2 H. Herrmann/K. Ahrens (Porsche 908)
3 G. Koch/H.-D. Dechent (Porsche 907)
Record lap: P. Rodriguez (Ferrari 312P), 2m. 48.1s., 134.402 m.p.h.

May 4—Targa Florio
1 G. Mitter/U. Schutz (Porsche 908), 6h. 7m. 45.3s., 73.42 m.p.h.
2 V. Elford/U. Maglioli (Porsche 908)
3 H. Herrmann/R. Stommelen (Porsche 908)
Record lap: Elford, 35m. 8.2s., 76.84 m.p.h.

May 11—Spa 1,000 km.
1 J. Siffert/B. Redman (Porsche 908), 4h. 24m. 19.6s., 131.2 m.p.h. (record)
2 P. Rodriguez/D. Piper (Ferrari 312P)
3 V. Elford/K. Ahrens (Porsche 908)
Record lap: Redman, 3m. 37.1s., 145.281 m.p.h.

June 1—Nürburgring 1,000 km.
1 J. Siffert/B. Redman (Porsche 908), 6h. 11m. 02.3s., 100.9 m.p.h.
2 R. Stommelen/H. Herrmann (Porsche 908)
3 V. Elford/K. Ahrens (Porsche 908)
Fastest lap: C. Amon (Ferrari 312P), 8m. 3.3s., 105.5 m.p.h.

June 14/15—Le Mans 24-hour race
1 J. Ickx/J. Oliver (Ford GT40), 129.4 m.p.h.
2 H. Herrmann/G. Larrousse (Porsche 908)
3 D. Hobbs/M. Hailwood (Ford GT40)
Fastest lap: V. Elford (Porsche 917), 3m. 27.2s., 146.26 m.p.h.

July 12—Watkins Glen Six-Hours
1 J. Siffert/B. Redman (Porsche 908), 111.19 m.p.h.
2 V. Elford/R. Attwood (Porsche 908)
3 R. Lins/J. Buzzetta (Porsche 908)
Fastest lap: Elford, 1m. 19.3s., 119.77 m.p.h.

August 10—Austrian Grand Prix
1 J. Siffert/K. Ahrens (Porsche 917), 5h. 23m. 36.98s.
2 J. Bonnier/H. Muller (Lola-Chevrolet T70 Mk. 3B)
3 R. Attwood/B. Redman (Porsche 917)
Fastest lap: J. Ickx (Ford GT40), 1m. 46.6s.

Manufacturers' Championship
1 Porsche   45 points
2 Ford   25
3 Lola-Chevrolet 20

GT Manufacturers' Championship
1 Porsche   45 points
2 Lola-Chevrolet 24
3 Ferrari   7

GUARDS FORMULA 5000 CHAMPIONSHIP
April 4—Oulton Park
1 P. Gethin (McLaren-Chevrolet M10A), 57m. 28s., 106.66 m.p.h.
2 D. Hobbs (Surtees TS5-Chevrolet)
3 K. Holland (Lola-Chevrolet T142)
Fastest lap: Gethin, 1m. 31.2s., 108.99 m.p.h.

April 7—Brands Hatch
1 P. Gethin (McLaren-Chevrolet M10A), 1h. 3m. 0.6s., 100.94 m.p.h.
2 K. Holland (Lola-Chevrolet T142)
3 W. Forbes (Lola-Chevrolet T142)
Fastest lap: Gethin, 1m. 31.6s., 104.15 m.p.h.

May 11—Brands Hatch
1 P. Gethin (McLaren-Chevrolet M10A), 1h. 7m. 13s., 90.76 m.p.h.
2 F. Gardner (Lola-Chevrolet T142)
3 K. Holland (Lola-Chevrolet T142)
Fastest lap: Gethin, 47s., 94.98 m.p.h.

May 26—Mallory Park
1 P. Gethin (McLaren-Chevrolet M10A), 1h. 2m. 53.6s., 103.03 m.p.h.
2 D. Hobbs (Surtees TS5-Chevrolet)
3 M. Walker (Lola-Chevrolet T142)
Fastest lap: Gethin, 44.0s., 110.45 m.p.h.

Gordon Spice leads the field in the British Saloon Car Championship at Crystal Palace. He stayed in front to the finish.

June 15—Silverstone

1 M. Walker (Lola-Chevrolet T142), 52m. 52.4s., 116.25 m.p.h.
2 A. Rollinson (Brabham-FVA BT30)
3 W. Forbes (Lola-Chevrolet T142)
Fastest lap: T. Taylor (Surtees TS5-Chevrolet), 1m. 26.8s., 121.39 m.p.h.

July 13—Rothmans Dublin Grand Prix, Mondello Park

1 D. Hobbs (Surtees TS5-Chevrolet), 1h. 23m. 35s.
2 M. Hailwood (Lola-Chevrolet T142)
3 A. Rollinson (Brabham-FVA BT30)
Fastest lap: Hobbs, 57.2s., 78.04 m.p.h.

August 3—North Sea Trophy, Koksijde, Belgium

1 T. Taylor (Surtees TS5-Chevrolet), 1h. 6m. 55s., 115.22 m.p.h.
2 A. Rollinson (Lola-Chevrolet T142)
3 K. Holland (Lola-Chevrolet T142)
Fastest lap: De Adamich (Surtees TS5-Chevrolet), 1m. 29.1s., 118.0 m.p.h.

August 10—Zandvoort 5000, Holland

1 T. Taylor (Surtees TS5-Chevrolet), 58m. 6.3s., 107.62 m.p.h.
2 P. Westbury (Brabham-FVA BT30)
3 M. Hailwood (Lola-Chevrolet T142)
Fastest lap: Taylor, 1m. 25.5s., 109.67 m.p.h.

September 1—Snetterton

1 T. Taylor (Surtees TS5-Chevrolet), 57m. 42.6s., 112.7 m.p.h.
2 M. Hailwood (Lola-Chevrolet T142)
3 M. Walker (Lola-Chevrolet T142)
Fastest lap: Taylor, 1m. 24.6s., 115.32 m.p.h.

September 14—Preis der Nationen, Hockenheim

1 T. Taylor (Surtees TS5-Chevrolet), 58m. 34.3s.
2 M. Hailwood (Lola-Chevrolet T142)
3 U. Norinder (Lola-Chevrolet T142)
Fastest lap: Taylor, 1m. 54.6s., 132.10 m.p.h.

Rosemary Smith (Escort Twin Cam) on her way to victory for the Ladies Prize in the 1969 Scottish Rally.

The Broadspeed Escort GT of John Fitzpatrick and Trevor Taylor which finished second in the Guards International 6-Hour European Championship Touring Car Race.

September 20—Oulton Park

1 M. Walker (Lola-Chevrolet T142), 1h. 3m. 10s., 104.9 m.p.h.
2 A. Rollinson (Lola-Chevrolet T142)
3 K. Holland (Lola-Chevrolet T142)
Fastest lap: Hailwood (Lola-Chevrolet T142), 1m. 31.2s., 108.99 m.p.h.

September 28—Brands Hatch

1 M. Hailwood (Lola-Chevrolet T142), 1h. 2m. 1.6s., 102.54 m.p.h.
2 A. Rollinson (Lola-Chevrolet T142)
3 K. Holland (Lola-Chevrolet T142)
Fastest lap: Hailwood, Taylor (Surtees TS5-Chevrolet) and Gethin (McLaren-Chevrolet M10A), 1m. 30.2s., 105.76 m.p.h.

Guards European Formula 5000 Championship

1 P. Gethin   2365 points
2 T. Taylor   2170
3 M. Hailwood   2045

CAN-AM SERIES
Final positions

1 B. McLaren   165 points
2 D. Hulme   160
3 C. Parsons   81

EUROPEAN TOURING CAR CHAMPION-SHIP

Division 3: D. Quester   42 points
Division 2: S. Dini   41
Division 1: 'Pam'   46

EUROPEAN HILL CLIMB CHAMPIONSHIP

1 P. Schetty   56 points
2 A. Merzario   38
3 M. Weber   21

EUROPEAN RALLY CHAMPIONSHIP
Rally Championship—Manufacturers

1 Ford Europe   33 points
2 Porsche   31
3 BMW   30

Rally Championship—Drivers

1 H. Kallstrom and G. Haggbom   59 points
3 G. Staepelaere and A. Aerts   51
5 C. Orrenius and S. Andreasson   16

OTHER EVENTS
Indianapolis 500-mile race

1 M. Andretti (Hawk-turbo-Ford)
2 D. Gurney (Eagle-Ford)
3 R. Unser (Lola-turbo-Offy)

RAC Tourist Trophy Race

1 T. Taylor (Lola-Chevrolet)
2 D. Piper (Lola-Chevrolet)
3 J. Miles (Lotus)

RAC WORLD RALLY CHAMPIONSHIP FOR MANUFACTURERS

1 Porsche
2 Lancia
3 Ford of Germany

RAC NATIONAL RALLY CHAMPIONSHIP

1 J. Bloxham (Ford-BRM)
2 J. Bullough (Ford)

The

Colin Chapman

Scrap-book

Colin Chapman, man behind the successful Lotus team, began building his cars in the backyard. Above: 1948—and the Austin-based Lotus Mk 1 nears completion. Chapman at the wheel. Below: 1949—Chapman and Hazel (now Mrs C) drive the Lotus Mk 11 in a 'mud-plugging' event. Meantime, Chapman graduated at London University, served in the RAF and worked at British Aluminium.

Colin Chapman, (above) at the wheel of the Lotus Mk VI, the first production model. The year was 1953. Below: four years on to 1957 and Cliff Allison drives the first Lotus single-seater Formula Two car, the Mk XII.

Above: 1960—Chapman in the white Jaguar at Becketts, Silverstone, overtaking Jack Sears. Below: 1963—Chapman rides down Victory Lane astride the rear of Jim Clark's Lotus 25. That year Chapman won the World Constructor's Championship and Clark the World Driver's Championship.

Above: 1968—the Oulton Park Gold Cup meeting. Graham Hill and the great Argentinian world champion, Juan Manuel Fangio, Colin Chapman and Henry Taylor. Below: 1969—part of the new Lotus factory near Norwich. Lotus are now one of the biggest manufacturers in Britain not controlled by America.

Above: 1969—Hazel Chapman, the girl behind Colin in his early backyard struggles to build cars, with Sarah, Clive and Jane, all set for a 'life on the ocean wave'. Below: 1969—and in contrast to the 1948 Mk I, the gleaming elegance of a two-seater Elan and an Elan Plus Two—with their creator.

In the 'twenties and 'thirties, international motor racing was dominated by the blood-red Alfa Romeos of Italy and the pale blue Bugattis of France. The star drivers too were mostly Italian and French save for the great British Grand Prix ace, Sir Henry Segrave. But one of the French-speaking members of the Bugatti equipe was not all that he seemed. Driving a Bugatti like the beautifully-preserved one shown above, he won many important races but few knew anything about him. Joan Drackett tells the story of the man who appeared in the programmes as . . .

JUST WILLIAMS

THE pilot watched the parachute blossom and open beneath him then turned his aircraft towards the Channel and England. It was a clear night—too clear—and the moon peered fitfully from behind the scudding clouds.

The pilot shivered. He was glad that he wasn't swinging and swaying beneath that silken canopy, watching the ground coming up steadily to meet him, wondering what awaited when he landed. . . .

Because the year was 1942 and his passenger was parachuting into France, into a land no longer gay and friendly but cold and hostile. Into a land ground under the heel of the German invader. Man of courage that he was himself, the pilot was constantly appalled at the temerity and bravery of those who

would leave the comparative safety of England for the unknown perils of enemy-occupied territory.

He was used to having strange passengers on these nocturnal expeditions but the man who had just left the 'plane was certainly an odd one. He'd hardly spoken a word from the time he had hurried across the airfield and climbed quickly into the machine but he had mentioned that he too was English; and yet he spoke with a strong French accent.

The pilot shook himself out of his reverie, pushed thoughts of the mystery man into the back of his head and concentrated on the task in hand. There would be other nights and other passengers and the night skies over France were no place to linger. . . .

It was 1926. At La Baule, seaside resort on the

coast of Brittany, the Grand Prix de Provence was to be held and had been honoured by the entry of the topnotch Anglo-French motor-racing equipe of Talbots. The Talbots did all that was expected of them when the race was run but many of the crowd reserved their cheers for a Bugatti driver, an unknown who hurled his car through corners with a daredevil recklessness which appealed to the Gallic temperament.

But dash and enthusiasm couldn't prevail against the cool experience of the Talbot aces and Britain's Henry Segrave streaked first across the line followed by his team-mate Jean Moriceau. The Bugatti was third. The driver's name was shown in the programme as 'Williams' but since it was given in quotes no one was very much wiser as to his real identity.

Who was he, this man who had made Europe's top racing drivers work so hard for victory? Where did he come from? The local inhabitants at least knew of him. He was a gentleman, monsieur. Yes, he lived in La Baule, monsieur. Oh yes, he is a Frenchman, monsieur.

And more than that none could say.

But his racing nom-de-plume, or whatever it was, gradually became known all over France. 'Williams' had a style which caught the fancy of the crowds. It did more. Le Patron, Ettore Bugatti himself, the most famous man in French motor-sport, was greatly impressed by the newcomer and lost no time in offering him a chance with the official Bugatti works team.

So 'Williams' came to England for the British Grand Prix which was held at Brooklands in 1927. As yet he was only a reserve driver but his opportunity came when one of the regular drivers, Conelli, collapsed with exhaustion, after his car had run out of petrol and he had pushed it all the way to the pits. In the best fiction, 'Williams' would have leaped into the car and roared to victory. In reality, he did nothing of the sort. In fact, in his wild enthusiam, he nearly crashed and the race was won by the rival French marque of Delage, the driver being Robert Benoist. The careers of Benoist and 'Williams' were to converge again under vastly different circumstances.

Le Patron was not discouraged by the failure of his new recruit. He was rarely wrong in his judg-

Then for a time, he was dogged by ill-health. Taking a corner too fast during practice for the Rome Grand Prix he crashed and as a result had to spend some time in hospital. The effects of his accident were not easily shaken off and he wasn't very successful during the following year, 1930.

But 1931 saw him back at his best with a convincing win in the Belgian Grand Prix against the cream of European racing drivers and cars. His co-driver was the same Conelli whose indisposition had given 'Williams' his chance at Brooklands.

Yet amidst all this success, 'Williams' remained a man of mystery. In pits and garages, bars and hotels, they talked and conjectured but none knew who he really was or from where he came.

The observing ones remarked that in the 'round-the-houses' race at Monaco, his Bugatti had been painted green, traditional racing colours of England, instead of the blue of France. But, darn it, man, the fellow speaks French like a native.

So it seemed that the mystery of 'Williams' would remain a mystery. The days when newspaper reporters were sent by their editors to get the human interest stories behind the news were not yet. Public curiosity into the private lives of the famous had to remain unsatisfied.

'Williams' himself had apparently no desire to lift the veil of secrecy which surrounded him. He continued about his affairs and those who came into contact with him shrugged their shoulders and minded their own business. After all, he was a good driver and his private life was nothing to do with anyone else.

So when he retired from racing to return to his home at La Baule, there to breed Aberdeen terriers, the world forgot him.

And there the story of 'Williams' might have ended with his secret undisclosed. But the Germans invaded France. And one of the consequences of their action was that 'Williams' was forced into revealing his true nationality and identity, something he had managed to conceal through all his years as an idol of the racing crowds.

He made his way to England, there to step into uniform as a British subject holding the King's Commission, Captain William Grover.

ment of a driver and he was not wrong this time. 'Williams' learned by his mistakes.

He commenced the following season by finishing second in the Circuit of Garoupe. A fine performance this for the winner was the Champion of Europe, the great Louis Chiron himself. Then came victory and first place with a works Bugatti in the French Grand Prix.

In 1929 he won the Monaco Grand Prix, a race which was graced with the honour of being the Grand Prix of Europe. 'Williams' followed up by repeating his success in the Fench Grand Prix, this time at Le Mans.

His strange, romantic story was by no means over.

A lifelong resident of France, speaking the language fluently, himself taken for a Frenchman by most of those who knew him, Grover (or 'Williams') obviously had exceptional qualities fitting him for the hazardous task of a special agent.

His courage was not in doubt. Had in fact been tested and proved on the race tracks of Europe a thousand times over. So he was given a period of intensive training, learning how to operate miniature radio transmitters, how to conceal messages, how to sabotage railways, blow-up ammunition dumps, organise underground resistance movements.

Then he was dropped into enemy territory. The years spent in France were of inestimable value to him now as he developed a network of communications and trained, and armed saboteurs and other resistance workers.

But something went wrong. Whether he was betrayed, whether his own assuredness and ease in playing the part of a Frenchman led him into making a careless slip, that is not known. What is known is that in 1943 he was captured by the Germans and imprisoned.

His work went on however. Earlier he had succeeded in contacting a friend of his racing days, that same Robert Benoist who had won the British Grand Prix at Brooklands in 1927. Benoist was soon enlisted in the Allied cause. He was also briefed in the wiles and guile of a special agent and one night, not long after the capture of 'Williams', a boat with muffled oars pulled into a lonely inlet on the French coast. From it stepped the courageous Benoist, eager and ready to continue the work of his captured friend and comrade.

Later, he too was captured and executed but not before he had done considerable harm to the Nazi cause. 'Williams' himself, there is reason to believe, was alive for some time after his capture but was shot following the D-Day landings.

His name and fate apart, the other mysteries surrounding 'Williams' remain. Twenty-five years after his death, the full story of his work, his capture and his death is not known with any certainty.

Nor is it known why he chose to live his life in France, why he raced under the name of 'Williams' and why he was content to let his friends and acquaintances think of him as a Frenchman.

We only know that he answered the call immediately when war was declared and died a soldier of his country working for the liberation of the nation which had welcomed him and harboured him for so many years.

Perhaps too, we can surmise that he would wish to be remembered, not as Captain William Grover, but more simply as just 'Williams'. . . .

Bugattis, Alfas and Maseratis at Monaco (below) and (opposite) a Bugatti in hot pursuit of a Maserati.